the
PASTA
FRIDAY
cookbook

the PASTA FRIDAY cookbook

ALLISON AREVALO

Over 70 recipes and tips to help
you start a weekly pasta tradition
that will change your life.

photography by
SARA REMINGTON

Andrews McMeel
PUBLISHING®

For
MOM AND DAD

TABLE OF CONTENTS

WHAT IS PASTA FRIDAY AND HOW TO START YOUR OWN TRADITION

"IT'S PASTA FRIDAY, IT'S PASTA FRIDAY!"

This is what my husband and I hear every Friday morning, around 7:00 a.m., when our two young boys barge into our room and start jumping on our bed. It's their favorite day of the week, because every Friday night our house is packed with close to fifty people, including friends, family, neighbors, and children. I cook a giant pot of pasta and make an equally giant salad, and our guests bring the wine. It's casual, with people grabbing pieces of fresh mozzarella from the counter and kids running around with thick, buttered slices of bread in hand (though half of them are feeding their bread to our dog). But mostly you'll find everyone laughing and relaxing after a long week and thankful that they don't have to cook dinner. Friends who I wouldn't normally see for months at a time now gather around my table every week. New bonds and new support systems are formed, and a new way to share meals (for this generation, at least). We call it Pasta Friday—and it changed our life.

HOW PASTA FRIDAY BECAME A THING

To start at the beginning means taking you back to Hewlett, New York, in the early nineties. The meatballs are frying on the stove and the pigskin simmering in the sauce, at my great-grandmother's house. Every week after church my family would gather for Sunday supper, a pasta feast prepared by a ninety-two-year-old woman who needed to stand on a stepstool to flip the meatballs. This was how my family, and many Italian families on Long Island, spent their Sundays. It was a glorious childhood made up of red sauce, plastic-covered couches, cousins, and cheek pinching.

But I grew up and moved across the country, and traditions faded. The Sunday suppers had instilled in me a love of food, community, and family—and the importance of having all these things in my life on a consistent basis. I dreamt of opening a business, a restaurant, incorporating these values. I just didn't know quite how to do it yet.

After years of working corporate marketing jobs, I took the leap and, with a friend, opened a restaurant in Oakland, California, dedicated to macaroni and cheese. We chose mac and cheese because we loved how it made people smile and because no one else in the Bay Area was doing it. This little mac and cheese restaurant turned out to be a huge success. I was featured on national media outlets, wrote a mac and cheese cookbook, and grew the business to two locations. It was a community gathering spot, a place where families went to celebrate special occasions and young couples had their first dates. I had two baby boys, a loving husband, and the restaurant

I always wanted. It was the kind of success most people only dream about.

But things changed. The restaurant grew into a big business. My days were filled with strategy meetings, workers' comp meetings, meetings about three-year plans, and meetings about meetings. I was miserable. I turned into an insomniac. I dreaded getting up in the morning to go to work, even though it was a company that I created.

So I left. I sold my shares and walked away from the business that I literally built from an empty shell.

It was one of the toughest decisions of my life, and I second-guessed myself, wondering if leaving a successful business in exchange for my sanity was the right thing to do. It was a dark time for me. Besides my anxiety over the business, my then four-year-old son, Nico, needed a risky surgery, and my sister was battling stage four cancer. The only time I felt better and stopped worrying was when I was cooking for my friends. So I invited them over every Friday for pasta. I made it official the week after my grandmother died at the end of August in 2017. It felt right to honor her memory by starting a tradition that promoted the values she instilled in me.

And it became a feast! Suddenly, I had one hundred people on my email list, and every week more and more people would show up, with bottles of wine in hand, excited to forget their own troubles and to connect with new people over heaping plates of pasta with Bolognese or pesto or clam sauce. Parents with young children would tell me it felt like a night out, a chance to socialize again. We were building a community, and our kids were, too! We suddenly had a list of people to call when we needed a last-minute babysitter, or a lead on a new job, or someone to listen when we wanted to vent about our day. And, we put our phones down. This was old-school interaction. Our fancy gadgets might as well have been Polaroids, because the only time we picked them up was to snap photos of the kids with sticky fingers or the mountains of pasta we were about to enjoy.

You don't have to cook for a crowd to reap the benefits of this tradition. Whether you're cooking for your family or just a few friends, the act of sitting together over a bowl of pasta can be transformational and healing. You'll get hooked. I guarantee it.

This cookbook is a collection of the recipes and stories that changed my life, and I think they'll change yours, too.

HOW TO START YOUR OWN PASTA FRIDAY

After hosting these gatherings for more than a year, I learned a few things that make cooking for a crowd easier. The most important tip I can give you, and one that may only be possible after you have a few of these dinners under your belt, is to relax. These dinners are meant to be casual gatherings of family and friends, not elegant dinner parties. Your table does not need to look like a Pinterest board!

You're making pasta and salad, and that's it—no appetizers and no desserts. The only dessert I allow are Popsicles for the kids. Also, it's okay if your laundry isn't folded. No one will mind if the food isn't ready as soon as they get there. I know it's hard; I'm a perfectionist, too, but it gets easier. Here's a list of other tricks I've learned along the way:

- **Setting expectations is the key.** Send out a weekly e-mail letting people know how to RSVP, what to bring (and more importantly, what not to bring), and what time to leave. I ask guests to bring a bottle of wine per adult, because people drink a lot when they're eating pasta, and I also ask for no desserts, other than Popsicles for the kids. The last thing I want is a pile of stale cookies left at my house. Lastly, I ask them to leave by 9:00 p.m.—because, you know . . . kids.

- **Know your limit.** Whether you want ten or fifty people, know your limit, and cut off the RSVPs when you hit it. You can do this by using an online sign-up sheet or by simply e-mailing the group when all the spots are filled.

- **Keep it casual.** This is not the dinner for your good china or fancy tablecloth. Use compostable plates and forks, and even aluminum trays for the salads, to make clean up easier. Or better yet, ask guests to bring their own plates! And you don't need seats for everyone. Guests don't mind standing and chatting while they're eating.

- **Don't accommodate dietary restrictions.** This is a slippery slope. I started out offering to make gluten-free pasta for a few guests, but that turned into requests for no dairy, no meat, extra meat, no sauce. Instead, I tell people to bring their own food if they have allergies or restrictions, and it works out great. My vegetarian friends bring their own sauce, my Keto friends bring chicken, and I don't have to stress about accommodating everyone.

- **If you're having a bunch of kids, feed them first.** This works best for two reasons: (1) The parents can relax and eat without worrying if their children are eating, and (2) You'll have more space at the table. I always make a big pot of penne with butter for the kids, although you will have the occasional overachiever who will eat the adult pasta.

- **Don't stress about tidiness.** The truth is no one is going to notice if you have Legos thrown in the corner or a pile of laundry on the bed. But:

  - **Keep the bathroom clean.** Make sure it's stocked with toilet paper, wipes for parents, and hand towels. Guests *will* notice the bathroom!

  - **Pre-clean.** Spend some time right before the guests arrive cleaning up the kitchen—wash the pots, wipe down the countertops. Guests would rather watch (and help) you cook then stand around in a dirty kitchen.

- **Set a weekly budget.** And stick to it! If you're getting close to hitting your limit, ask guests to chip in by picking up grated cheese, pasta for the kids, or baguettes. I usually put a quick post up on my Pasta Friday Facebook group to see who can help out.

- **Use an online delivery service if you don't have time to shop.** That way, when you get home from work, your groceries are waiting for you.

- **Don't save the cleanup for the next day.** Get people to help out, or just knock it out when everyone leaves. You'll thank me Saturday morning.

PREPARING FOR PASTA FRIDAY

The great thing (well, one of the great things) about pasta is that it's relatively inexpensive. You can buy quality ingredients that feed a lot of people for much less money than a typical dinner party, especially because you're not preparing appetizers or desserts. **All you're serving is pasta and salad. That's it.**

Because it helps to know what to shop for when starting a weekly pasta tradition, I put together a list of a few basics that I usually have on hand. There's nothing crazy or exotic or too hard to find, especially if you have an Italian specialty store nearby. You probably have most of these items in your pantry already. So here it is, a guide to ingredients to always have on hand:

DRIED PASTA

Most of the time you'll be buying dried pasta, right? Because who has time to roll out pasta dough on a Friday night after work? Definitely not me. But let me tell you why it's worth splurging on the more expensive brands of pasta.

When you look at pasta labels, you want to see that the pasta is cut with bronze dies. This means that when the pasta dough comes out of the giant extruder, it's cut into different shapes with a circular, bronze die that fits on the end of the machine. The bronze gives the pasta a rough surface, so the sauce sticks to it and gets absorbed into the pasta, instead of just sliding off. Sometimes you'll also see long drying times listed on the label. When the pasta is dried slowly, it doesn't break or crack easily. It helps the pasta keep its shape and texture when it's cooking, something that's really important when you're serving family-style and the pasta is sitting in the sauce for a few minutes. And if there are more than two ingredients (semolina and water), don't buy it.

When you buy well-made, artisan pasta, it becomes part of the dish—not just a vehicle for the sauce. Once you try it, you'll be able to easily tell it apart from the budget brands, probably even by looking at it. One of my favorite pasta companies is Rustichella d'Abruzzo, made in Italy. I visited their factory in Abruzzo and learned how to make pasta from them, and their efficiency and attention to detail were incredible! But there are many other great brands, like Martelli, or De Cecco for a lower-cost option. Do a quick search online to see if there are any local pasta makers in your area—you'll be surprised by how many there are.

OLIVE OILS

I have a slight obsession with extra-virgin olive oil. I always have at least five bottles on hand, eight if you count the flavored oils like chili, lemon, and orange.

That sounds like a lot, doesn't it? I have a specific use for all of them! You probably don't need quite that many, but I do think you need at least three oils on hand. Here's how they break down:

- **Olive oil for cooking:** A mild, fruity, extra-virgin olive oil is ideal for cooking. I usually buy a three-liter can because it's the best value, and I try to buy brands that have 100% Italian olives, rather than a blend of olives from different countries. Whole Foods, though, has a great, inexpensive three-liter blend under their 365 label. Partanna's three-liter can is also good for cooking.

- **Olive oil for pesto and salad dressings:** This is a step up from your cooking oil. Salad dressings and pesto use up a lot of oil, and while I would love to use the expensive stuff, I can't always afford it. For your mid-range oil, look for one that's silky, slightly bitter, robust, and has a bottling date on it. I'm drawn to Southern Italian oils, especially those from Sicily, Abruzzo, or Puglia, but I've also had some amazing oils from Spain, Greece, and California. California Olive Ranch has a nice mid-range oil made from Arbequina olives. The Columela brand from Spain is also one of my go-to oils when I'm making a big batch of salad dressing.

- **Olive oil for finishing:** This is your expensive stuff. I love finishing oil that's delicate but still somehow bold, with layers and layers of flavor. When you drizzle it on a salad or pasta, the taste of fresh olives stands apart from the sauce and cheese, and you get a hint of pepper at the back of your throat. A few of my favorites are Tondo from Sicily, Intosso from Abruzzo, and the Olio Nuovo from Calivirgin in California, which is seasonal and comes out every November. Once in a while when I'm cooking for my family, I'll splurge and make the entire dish with fancy olive oil, and holy cow, you can absolutely tell the difference.

SALT AND SPICES

If I'm being honest here, I can say that I don't use many dried spices. You'll notice when you start cooking these recipes, I don't ask you to go out and buy a ton of spice jars that end up sitting in your cabinet and going stale. But there are a few

essentials that are so essential, in fact, that I travel with a few of them and bring them on picnics. My boys give me an eye roll, but they're always happy when they can sprinkle flaky sea salt on their sliced cucumber.

For Pasta Friday dinners and weeknight cooking, I rely on good salts, quality black pepper, fresh herbs, and various chiles for spice. I keep things like dried oregano, smoked paprika, and ground cumin on hand, but not much else.

Salt

There aren't many things that can ruin a good meal like too much salt can. I rarely measure salt. I add a little, taste, and add more. Isn't it slightly irritating, though, when people say the water should "taste like the sea"? What does that even mean? I do my best to be accurate when talking about salt in my recipes, but different kinds of salts have varying saltiness. If you use a store-brand sea salt instead of kosher salt, for example, the amounts in my recipes may make the dishes too salty.

> **For salting pasta water, my rule of thumb is: two tablespoons of kosher salt per one pound of pasta.**

I make one to two pounds of pasta in a six-quart pot, but for anything more than that, I use at least a ten-quart pot.

Whenever you're not sure how much salt to add, make sure you add it slowly, tasting as you go. Here are the types of salt I use and when I use them. (Notice that iodized table salt is not on this list. I never use the stuff; it's too salty):

> **Kosher salt:** My go-to salt. I use fine kosher salt for cooking, salting pasta water, seasoning meat, salad dressings—almost everything. Kosher salt is not overly salty, if that makes sense.

> **Flaky sea salt:** I'm not quite as obsessed with flaky sea salt as I am with olive oil,

but it's close. I knew I had a problem when Luca, at four years old, said he only wanted to use Icelandic sea salt. I love how many different kinds of salt exist and how different they all taste. Some, like Maldon, have long, lean flakes that almost melt in your mouth. Others, like fleur de sel, have smaller grains and feel wet, like it was just harvested from the sea. Experiment with different kinds to see what you like best, but always have some on hand to use for finishing, in the same way you would use fancy olive oil.

Black Pepper

I feel the same way about black peppercorns as I feel about coffee beans. If they're not freshly ground, it's not worth bothering to use them. I'm sure you've heard this before, but just in case: Don't buy pre-ground black pepper. It tastes like paper. I use Tellicherry black peppercorns, because they're big and give the best peppery punch, and I usually coarsely grind them. If you're feeling ambitious, you can even use a mortar and pestle to grind your peppercorns, especially if you're making Cacio e Pepe (page 68). Unlike salt, I'll rarely give you an exact measurement for pepper, mostly because pepper levels are a personal preference. I go heavy on the pepper, but since I don't know what type of pepper you're using or how coarsely you're grinding it, I generally say "a few grinds" and leave it to you to decide how much pepper you want.

Fresh Herbs

I've been told I have a heavy hand with herbs, and I'm okay with that. If you were at Pasta Friday, you would see my giant pots of pasta completely covered in chopped herbs. I generally don't mince them, either. I like to bite into big leaves and fully taste them, especially in salads. If you have fresh herbs, a lemon, spaghetti, and olive oil, a great meal is only fifteen minutes away. I mix them up, often adding handfuls of basil, cilantro, parsley, and mint to the same dish.

Chiles

I take chiles seriously. I'm a spice fiend, and I like to have options when it comes to heat. On the Pasta Friday table, I'll often put at least three different types of hot peppers: dried red chili flakes, chiles in oil, and fresh hot peppers.

Dried red chili flakes: If you buy these at the supermarket, they're often brown, dull, and mild. Look for them at spice shops or specialty markets, and only buy them if they look bright red. You can also make your own: Buy some dried hot peppers, like cayenne peppers, and blitz them in a food processor or grind them with a mortar and pestle.

Chiles in oil: People go nuts for these chiles at Pasta Friday! I buy a jar of crushed Calabrian chiles in olive oil, usually the Tutto Calabria brand, and the jar is empty by the end of the night. Look for brands that don't add extra preservatives; there should be two ingredients—peppers and oil. You can find them at a specialty Italian store or online.

Fresh, minced peppers: A trick I learned from my great-grandmother is to always have a small bowl of minced jalapeños on the table, sometimes on their own, sometimes covered in olive oil. The crunchy kick is completely different in flavor and texture from the other chiles, and they add freshness to even the heartiest meat sauces.

CHEESE

I could write an entire book about cheese and pasta, but for now I'm going to focus on a particular type of cheese: hard, grating cheese.

I always have a wedge of something in the fridge: Pecorino Romano, Grana Padano, or Parmigiano-Reggiano. Pecorino is a hard sheep's-milk cheese that tends to be saltier and sharper than Parmigiano-Reggiano or Grana Padano, which are both cow's-milk cheeses with nuttier flavors. Grana Padano is great and worth trying. It's a little cheaper than Parmigiano-Reggiano and usually not aged as long, so it melts slightly better. But you can use Parmigiano-Reggiano and Grana Padano interchangeably.

I'm going to be honest, and don't think less of me, but I rarely use my best cheese for Pasta Friday, unless the cheese is a crucial element of the dish—Zero Ricotta Baked Ziti (page 26), Impress-Your-Friends Fettuccine Alfredo (page 147), or Cacio e Pepe (page 68), as a few examples. If I'm buying cheese for over twenty people to sprinkle on their pasta, I get a container of Italian pre-grated cheese from the market. But (and this is a big but) I buy imported grated cheese that was grated by the cheese department in that store. It's less expensive than a wedge of Parmigiano-Reggiano and still pretty tasty. Just stay away from the stuff that comes in a green can. Is that even real cheese?

For everyday cooking, I grate my own cheese. The only reason I don't for Pasta Friday is because of cost—good Pecorino or Parmigiano-Reggiano is around $20 per pound. I would rather spend that money on quality pasta, good olive oil, and organic meats than on grated cheese. Honestly, many of these dishes don't even need the extra cheese, but people love having the option to add it.

Speaking of grating, here's another trick: When you're grating hard cheese for pasta, use the second smallest side of your box grater or a microplane. The cheese will feel like snow falling on your pasta, gradually melting into the dish as you eat it. I think technically this is called "shredding," but whenever I grate cheese, that's how I do it.

CANNED TOMATOES

I only use whole, peeled, canned San Marzano tomatoes. They're the most versatile—you can chop, crush, and purée them. They taste the closest to fresh tomatoes, and they don't have preservatives added like some diced or crushed tomatoes. I like to break them up with my hands right before adding them to the pot (you'll see, I do that a lot), but you can also use a wooden spoon or chop them if you don't like getting your hands dirty. I use the juice in the can, too, but sometimes I like to caramelize the tomatoes before adding it.

Do you want to hear about an epic Pasta Friday fail on my part? One Friday, when I was having thirty-eight adults and twenty-five children over, I bought a new brand of San Marzano tomatoes, because they were on sale at the store. I bought five 28-ounce cans, brought them home, and started preparing the sauce. I was so stressed because of the crazy amount of people coming over, I forgot to taste the tomatoes before making the sauce. Well, ten minutes before everyone arrived, I remembered to taste my now-completed sauce, and it tasted LIKE KETCHUP. I almost cried (actually, I did cry). The lesson here is to always taste your tomatoes first. And oh, make sure they don't say "San Marzano-Style" tomatoes. It's not the same thing!

HOW TO USE THESE RECIPES AND SCALE THEM UP FOR A CROWD

I grew up in an Italian American family, fully immersed in Italian traditions, with recipes passed down from my grandmothers. I've traveled throughout Italy many times and learned a lot about traditional Italian cooking. However, **this book is not an "authentic" Italian cookbook,** although some recipes fall into that category. My cooking combines my upbringing with years of living on both coasts of the United States. I primarily use local, organic ingredients, but I'm not obsessive about it, because not going broke is also important. I don't like chemicals or ingredients I can't pronounce, so I stay away from highly processed foods. I'm not afraid to throw in extra heat, extra cheese, and extra olive oil. This is not a low-fat cookbook.

I hope you'll use these recipes for gatherings around the table with family and friends and see that I make it slightly less scary to host a crowd on a regular basis.

52 WEEKS, 52 SHAPES OF PASTA: A Recipe for Every Week of the Year!

I've always been fascinated by the different types of pasta available, so when I started Pasta Friday, I set the goal of doing **fifty-two dinners, fifty-two different recipes, fifty-two pasta shapes.** That's a recipe for every week of the year, each with a different shape! Experimenting with these shapes was eye-opening. Some shapes are hard to find, so every recipe will have recognizable, easier-to-find alternatives at the top of the page, below the wine pairings. But if you have the time, search online or at Italian specialty shops to find the more obscure shapes—your guests will love it!

SCALING UP

It's easy to adapt these recipes to however many people you're cooking for each week, whether it's your family of four or a crowd of twenty. You'll notice each pasta recipe calls for one pound of pasta, which generally feeds four to six people, depending on how hungry they are and what else is in the recipe. The Lamb Ragù (page 134), for example, will feed more people than the Roasted Red Pepper Sauce (page 18). My portions are big. Some books say twelve ounces of pasta feeds around six people, but in my family, that's impossible.

Want to make the Garlicky Conchiglioni with Spinach and Cheese (page 102) for only two people on a weeknight? Or maybe Gemelli with Blistered Tomatoes and Balsamic Butter (page 31) for a gathering of ten people? Below are some guidelines I follow. Keep in mind the ratio of people to pounds of pasta isn't an exact correlation. When you have a large dinner party and people are laughing, chatting, and drinking, they tend to eat less than when it's a few people sitting around a table. If you're making a chunky, meaty, or creamy sauce, you can use less pasta, since the sauce is filling. And those are the best sauces for some bread dipping! These amounts also assume that you're making a salad with the pasta and that you'll have bread for people to pass around.

SERVINGS		DRIED PASTA
2 people	=	½ pound
4-6 people	=	1 pound
7-10 people	=	2 pounds
10-15 people	=	3 pounds
15-20 people	=	4 pounds
20-25 people	=	5 pounds

Remember that we're not baking here. It doesn't take a degree in chemistry to successfully scale up these recipes. Try, though, to always make slightly more than you think you'll need. It's better to end up with leftovers than to have guests leave hungry! Here are some guidelines for scaling up sauces:

Tomato-Based Sauces

My basic tomato sauce has three key elements: tomatoes, onions, and garlic. If I'm making a tomato sauce for my family of four, I use:

1 (28-ounce) can whole, peeled San Marzano tomatoes

1 large white onion
2 cloves garlic

This is a solid amount of sauce for one pound of pasta. As you scale up and add more pounds of pasta, the number of pounds should correlate to the number of cans of tomatoes, and the onions and garlic increase accordingly. So if you're making sauce for fourteen people, you would want to triple the recipe:

3 (28-ounce) cans whole, peeled San Marzano tomatoes

3 large white onions
6 cloves garlic

Meat-Based Sauces

These sauces aren't as clear-cut as the tomato-based sauce, because it depends on the type of meat you're using. For example, if I'm making spaghetti and meatballs, I estimate about four meatballs per person. When making a quick ragù with ground meat, I estimate one pound of meat for every four people. And if I'm slow-cooking or braising big hunks of meat, I never make less than three pounds at a time, even if I'm only feeding four people. If I'm going to the trouble of cooking meat for many hours, I like to have leftovers to use in other dishes.

Cream-Based Sauces

If you want to scale up cream sauces, don't just add more heavy cream. We've all had those restaurant experiences, whether it's vodka sauce, Alfredo, or lemon cream. The sauce tastes like all cream, and it's the worst. The job of cream in these sauces is to create a silky texture, a richness to hold the sauce together. If you try to stretch the sauce by just adding more cream, you'll be disappointed. To stretch a cream sauce, add more of the ingredients that give it flavor first. For example, when I make the Roasted Red Pepper Sauce (page 18) for a crowd of ten people, I roast five pounds of peppers and slowly add more cream until the sauce is a deep orange color, instead of just increasing the amount of cream in the recipe.

WINE PAIRINGS

All the pasta recipes have simple, suggested wine pairings for both white and red wines. For my dinners, I ask guests to bring a bottle of wine per adult. That seems like a lot of wine, right? When I first started Pasta Friday, I asked for only one bottle per couple, and every week we'd have to dig into our own stash. Now that each couple brings two bottles, my wine stash remains (relatively) intact.

What I also discovered, other than that people drink A LOT while eating pasta, is that most people brought what they like to drink, regardless of the menu. Some guests would bring my weekly menu to the wine shop for recommendations (which was awesome), and others would bring the same bottle of white wine every week because that's what they like. So, even though you may think it's against all the rules to drink white wine with spaghetti and meatballs, the "rules" don't apply on Pasta Friday. It's your night, drink what you like! I am not a sommelier, and I don't talk about any specific winemakers. These are simply recommendations based on my many years of drinking wine and eating pasta.

PASTA FRIDAY BY SEASON

This book is set up so you can start your own Pasta Friday tradition and have a recipe for every week of the year. You can start at the beginning, in the summer, or maybe in the fall when the weather is changing. Or maybe it's a New Year's resolution and you're starting in January. Whenever you decide to start, the recipes will be waiting for you, **fifty-two pasta recipes and sixteen salads, so you can have a full year of dinners.**

Remember to enjoy it. Our grandmothers didn't stress when they prepared big meals for the family. They weren't trying to impress people on social media with photos of fancy new napkin holders (although maybe they should have taken the plastic off the couch). This is about getting to see your friends and family every week and building a community. Relax, it's Pasta Friday!

SUMMER

Pasta Friday during the summer means pounds of fresh tomatoes, sweet corn, stone fruit, and lots of basil. The kids play outside long past their bedtime, enjoying every last second of daylight. The grown-ups sip cold white wine and eat slowly. There's no rush during the summer—even the tech execs relax and stay later than usual. There are fewer people, because everyone is away on their summer holiday, and that's okay. The smaller crowds are more intimate and cut down on the time spent cooking and cleaning!

SUMMER PASTA

Bucatini with Summer Corn and Pancetta 16

Rigatoncini with Roasted Heirloom Tomatoes and Pesto 17

Dad's Famous Roasted Red Pepper Sauce 18

Crispy Casarecce with Tuna, Tomatoes, and Arugula 21

Pam's Pasta with Sausage, Tomatoes, and Peaches 23

Rigatoni with Bacon and Tomatoes 25

Zero Ricotta Baked Ziti 26

Whole-Wheat Thin Spaghetti with Zucchini and Onions 28

Gemelli with Blistered Tomatoes and Balsamic Butter 31

Tagliatelle with Ricotta Sauce and Fried Squash Blossoms 32

Farfalloni with Smoked Salmon and Creamy Corn Sauce 34

Stefania's Paccheri Fragola with Mozzarella and Crispy Basil 37

Trofie with Pesto Cream, Potatoes, and Green Beans 39

SUMMER SALADS

Grandma's Simple Tomato Salad with Buttery Crostini 41

Cucumber Basil Salad with Anchovies and Croutons 42

Classic Chopped Italian Salad 43

Butter Lettuce with Prosciutto, Peaches, and Burrata 45

Bucatini with Summer Corn and Pancetta

SERVES 4 TO 6

Wine Pairings

RED: soft, fruity Oregon pinot noir

WHITE: herbaceous, floral California sauvignon blanc

PASTA SHAPES: spaghettoni, pici, pasta al ceppo

SERVE WITH: extra breadcrumbs, dried red chili flakes

If you're starting at the beginning and this is your first Pasta Friday, then woohoo! You're in luck, because not only is this the dish I make when I want my cooking to make a good first impression, it comes together quickly. It represents everything that's great about summer, twirled around thick and chewy bucatini. Don't forget the breadcrumbs; their extra crunch is exactly what this dish needs!

Every week I make penne with butter for the kids to eat, but this week nearly all of the kids preferred the "adult" pasta. The magical combo of pancetta and corn pleases all ages!

Kosher salt

¼ cup extra-virgin olive oil

8 ounces pancetta, diced

4 cups fresh or frozen and thawed corn kernels

Freshly ground black pepper

4 cloves garlic, minced

1 pound bucatini

3 tablespoons salted butter, diced

1½ pounds medium, ripe tomatoes (such as Early Girls), coarsely chopped

1 cup coarsely chopped fresh basil leaves

1 cup Spicy Breadcrumbs (page 160)

12 ounces burrata, room temperature

High-quality olive oil, for drizzling

1   Fill a 6-quart pot with water. Bring it to a boil and add 2 tablespoons of salt. While the water is coming to a boil, heat the olive oil in a large, heavy pot over medium-high heat. Add the pancetta and cook for 6 to 8 minutes, until browned and crispy. Remove the pancetta with a slotted spoon, leaving the rendered fat in the pot. Add the corn, 1 teaspoon of salt, and a few grinds of black pepper. Cook, without stirring, for 4 minutes, then stir and cook for another 3 minutes, until the corn has slightly browned. Add the garlic and cook for about 1 minute more.

2   Add the pasta to the boiling water and cook until slightly firmer than al dente, 1 minute less than what it says on the package. Using tongs, transfer the pasta to the pot with the corn. Add the pancetta, butter, tomatoes, basil, and ½ cup of the pasta cooking water, and toss well. Add the breadcrumbs and toss again. Add a few more tablespoons of the cooking water if it looks dry.

3   Pour into a serving dish. Tear apart the burrata and scatter it on top. Drizzle with fancy olive oil and serve immediately.

Rigatoncini with Roasted Heirloom Tomatoes and Pesto

SERVES 4 TO 6

Wine Pairings
RED: medium-bodied, slightly sweet Italian dolcetto
WHITE: bright, acidic Portuguese albariño

PASTA SHAPES: penne, paccheri, capellini

SERVE WITH: extra pesto, grated Parmigiano-Reggiano

Recipe Note
This works well with regular tomatoes in place of heirloom tomatoes, for a thicker, less brothy sauce. Also try a mix of heirloom and regular tomatoes if you want a sauce somewhere in the middle.

The ratio of sauce to pasta is very much a personal preference, although plenty of purists will tell you the pasta should never look like it's swimming. Perfectly sauced pasta means the sauce sticks to the noodles and you're not left with a pool of sauce when you're done.

This is not that sauce. Heirloom tomatoes generally let out a lot of liquid, so when you're making a fresh sauce with them, unless you're straining the juice and seeds or using tomato paste, you're left with a fragrant, bright, intensely flavored tomato broth that is begging to be sopped up with fresh bread or slurped with a spoon.

4 pounds mixed heirloom tomatoes, cored and left whole
1 large white onion, halved and thinly sliced into half moons
3 cloves garlic, thinly sliced
¼ cup extra-virgin olive oil

Kosher salt
Freshly ground black pepper
1 pound rigatoncini
½ cup basic pesto (page 162)
Freshly grated Parmigiano-Reggiano, for serving

1 Preheat the oven to 350°F.

2 Arrange the tomatoes in a single layer in a large roasting pan. Snuggle the onions and garlic around the tomatoes. Drizzle the olive oil over the vegetables, and season with 1 teaspoon of salt and a few grinds of pepper. Cook for 45 minutes, until the tomatoes release their juices. Remove from the oven and cool to the touch. Remove and discard the skins from the tomatoes. Gently break the tomatoes apart and place them back into the pan with the onions and garlic. Turn the oven off and place the sauce in the oven to keep it warm while you make the pasta.

3 Fill a 6-quart pot with water. Bring it to a boil and add 2 tablespoons of salt. Add the pasta, and stir. Cook until slightly firmer than al dente, 1 minute less than it says on the package, and drain.

4 Pour the pasta back into the pot, and pour the sauce over the pasta. Cook over low heat for 2 minutes, until the pasta is fully cooked, stirring occasionally. Transfer to a large bowl. Spoon the pesto and some grated cheese on top.

Dad's Famous Roasted Red Pepper Sauce

SERVES 4 TO 6

Wine pairings

RED: medium-bodied, spicy California cabernet franc

WHITE: unoaked, crisp French Chardonnay

PASTA SHAPES: penne, gemelli, radiatore

SERVE WITH: Crispy, Spicy Prosciutto (page 161), grated Parmigiano-Reggiano

We would beg, BEG, my dad to make this sauce. My sister, Lenore, and I would cause such a scene that he would have no choice but to say yes. Then we'd call Jen, the neighborhood girl who practically lived at our house, and tell her to run over quick because Dad was making "the sauce." We wouldn't have to say which one. She knew.

There are a couple of tricks to this sauce that help make the sweetness from the peppers pop. First, don't rinse them after you roast them. Second, go easy on the cream. The amount of cream listed here works well for three pounds of peppers, but still, keep an eye on the color of the sauce. You want a bright, bold, orangey pink, not a muted mauve. Make it as spicy as you like, or omit the cayenne chiles if you prefer mild. Marash pepper also works nicely in this sauce.

3 pounds red bell peppers, roasted, peeled, and seeded (recipe follows)

2 cups heavy cream

8 tablespoons salted butter

1 tablespoon roasted garlic (recipe follows)

1 teaspoon smoked paprika

1 teaspoon ground cayenne chile or Marash pepper

Kosher salt

1 pound cannolicchi

1 Purée the roasted peppers with the heavy cream in a blender or food processor, working in batches if necessary.

2 Melt the butter in a large, heavy pot over medium-low heat. Whisk the roasted garlic into the butter. Add the smoked paprika, chile pepper, and 1 teaspoon of salt. Cook for 1 minute, stirring, until it smells outrageously good.

3 Add the puréed peppers to the pot and stir. Decrease the heat to low and simmer for 10 to 15 minutes, stirring occasionally. Taste for salt and add more if needed.

4 While the sauce is cooking, fill a 6-quart pot with water and bring it to a boil. Add 2 tablespoons of salt, and then add the pasta and stir. Cook until the pasta is slightly firmer than al dente, 1 minute less than it says on the package, and drain. Add the pasta directly to the pot with the sauce, and gently stir to fully coat the pasta. Cook for 1 to 2 minutes, until the pasta is cooked al dente. Serve family-style right from the pot!

RECIPE CONTINUES ↓

ROASTED PEPPERS

1 Preheat the broiler, and position a rack about 6 inches from the heat.

2 Place the red bell peppers on a baking sheet, drizzle them with olive oil, and sprinkle with kosher salt. Broil the peppers for about 6 minutes, or until the skins are completely charred. Flip them over and broil for another 6 minutes.

3 When the skins are all black, transfer the peppers to a brown paper bag. Close up the bag to help steam the peppers and loosen the skins. When they're cool enough to handle, remove the stems, seeds, and skins, and coarsely chop. To store the peppers, cover with olive oil and refrigerate for up to 1 week.

ROASTED GARLIC

Preheat the oven to 325°F. Cut the top third off a head of garlic and discard. Place the garlic, cut side up, on a small sheet of aluminum foil, drizzle with olive oil, and season with salt. Close the foil around the garlic and roast, cut side up, for about 45 minutes. You'll know it's done when you open the package and the garlic is caramelized and soft. Squeeze the garlic cloves into a small bowl. To store, cover in olive oil and refrigerate for up to 1 week.

Crispy Casarecce with Tuna, Tomatoes, and Arugula

SERVES 4 TO 6

Wine Pairings
RED: fruity, homemade sangria
WHITE: bubbly, dry Italian prosecco

PASTA SHAPES: gemelli, strozzapreti, penne

SERVE WITH: minced jalapeño peppers, extra-virgin olive oil for drizzling

Have you ever heated up leftover pasta in a hot pan with olive oil and let it get all slick and crispy? This is basically the story of my life. I am always eating leftover pasta.

But I rarely think to intentionally make crispy pasta, even though I crave it whenever I see last night's pasta dinner in the fridge. If you're making this for a crowd, you can crisp up the pasta on a baking sheet in the oven or in batches on the stovetop. If you want to get fancy, shave a little bottarga on top.

Kosher salt

1 pound casarecce

1 pint cherry tomatoes, halved crosswise

2 cloves garlic, mashed into a paste

6 ounces Italian or Spanish tuna packed in oil, drained, and pulled apart

6 ounces nocellara or other large green olive, pitted and chopped

1 tablespoon finely grated lemon zest

3 ounces wild arugula

2 tablespoons coarsely chopped fresh cilantro

2 tablespoons unsalted butter

4 tablespoons extra-virgin olive oil, divided

Freshly ground black pepper

1 Fill a 6-quart pot with water. Bring it to a boil and add 2 tablespoons of salt. Cook the pasta until slightly firmer than al dente, 1 minute less than it says on the package. Drain, and run it under cold water. Line a baking sheet with paper towels, and spread the pasta on top to dry it out. The drier it is, the better it'll crisp up!

2 Meanwhile, combine the tomatoes, garlic, tuna, olives, lemon zest, arugula, and cilantro in a large bowl.

3 Melt the butter in your largest skillet over medium-high heat. Add 2 tablespoons of the olive oil, and when it's hot, add the pasta. Cook for 3 minutes without stirring, then stir it around, and cook for another 3 minutes, until the pasta is slightly brown and crisp. Pour the pasta into the large bowl, right on top of the sauce, and add the remaining 2 tablespoons of olive oil. Toss it all together. Taste for salt and add a few grinds of black pepper. Serve immediately.

Pam's Pasta with Sausage, Tomatoes, and Peaches

SERVES 6 TO 8

Wine Pairings
RED: light, slightly sweet
Italian lambrusco
WHITE: refreshing, mostly dry
German Riesling

PASTA SHAPES: campanelle, penne, fusilli

SERVE WITH: grated aged Manchego cheese, dried red chili flakes

Let me tell you all about Pam Mazzola. Pam is undoubtedly one of the best chefs in the Bay Area, but you wouldn't know it, because she is so incredibly humble, and instead of bragging on social media, she's running a business, raising a family, and helping her friends. Pam is the chef and co-owner of the renowned San Francisco restaurant Prospect, and she's co-author of Boulevard: The Cookbook. *She's also one of the most selfless, caring friends I've ever had. Pam's pasta has tomatoes AND peaches! Some of the peaches get tossed into the sauce, but don't forget to save the rest for garnish. I'm not sure why more recipes don't combine peaches and tomatoes. Once you try it, you won't know either.*

2 (28-ounce) cans whole, peeled San Marzano tomatoes, with juices

3 tablespoons extra-virgin olive oil

2 medium red onions, halved lengthwise and thinly sliced crosswise

12 ounces spicy Italian sausage, casing removed, crumbled

4 cloves garlic, finely chopped

1 tablespoon tomato paste

¾ cups dry white wine

Kosher salt

1 pound torchio pasta

¼ cup chiffonade fresh basil

2 peaches (ripe but not soft), sliced into ⅓-inch wedges, leaving the skin on

Dried red chili flakes (optional)

Freshly grated Manchego cheese, for serving

1 Strain the cans of tomatoes in a colander over a bowl. Set aside 1 cup of the juices, and reserve the rest for another use. Gently tear the tomatoes in half and squeeze out the seeds into the colander. Press out any remaining juice, setting aside for later, and chop the tomatoes.

2 Heat the olive oil in a large sauté pan over medium heat. Add the onions and gently cook until soft and beginning to caramelize, about 10 minutes. Increase the heat to medium-high and add the broken-up sausage, stirring to break it up further. Cook for about 8 minutes, until lightly browned, then add the garlic and tomato paste, and stir for 1 minute, until caramelized. Add the chopped tomatoes, the reserved cup of

RECIPE CONTINUES ↓

tomato juice, and the wine, and bring to a simmer, stirring occasionally. Cook for 10 minutes, uncovered, then cover the pan and cook over low heat for an additional 20 minutes.

3   While the sauce is cooking, fill a 6-quart pot with water and bring it to a boil. Add 2 tablespoons of salt, and then add the pasta and stir. Cook until the pasta is slightly firmer than al dente, 1 minute less than it says on the package, and drain.

4   Add the pasta to the sauce with the basil and two-thirds of the peaches. Toss well and season with salt and dried chili flakes, if you prefer spicy. Cook for 1 minute longer, then pour into a serving dish. Place the remaining peaches on top for garnish before serving, along with grated cheese.

Rigatoni with Bacon and Tomatoes

SERVES 4 TO 6

Wine Pairings
RED: earthy, leathery Italian primitivo
WHITE: dry, full-bodied Italian pinot grigio

PASTA SHAPES: penne, mezze paccheri, bucatini

SERVE WITH: minced jalapeño peppers, grated Parmigiano-Reggiano

I use bacon. I use pancetta. I use guanciale. Although they're similar (because, yeah, they're all pork), they are not the same! When it comes to pasta, here's what you need to know: When you cook with bacon, the entire dish will taste smoky and "bacon-y". When you cook with pancetta, the meaty flavor is contained in the actual pieces of pancetta, so the whole dish doesn't taste smoky. As for guanciale, this one is all about the rendered fat that gives the pasta a silky coating and the small pieces of pork that resemble crispy prosciutto. I love bacon in this recipe, because every bite of tomato and pasta has a hint of smoke and salt, but you can try it with all three.

8 ounces thick-cut bacon
Kosher salt
1 pound rigatoni
2 tablespoons extra-virgin olive oil

2 cloves garlic, minced
2½ pounds medium, ripe, red tomatoes, cut into wedges
Freshly ground black pepper
2 fresh egg yolks

1 Place the bacon in a large skillet over medium-high heat. Cook for 5 minutes, flip, and cook for another 3 minutes, until it's crispy but not burnt. Remove with tongs and place on a plate lined with paper towels. Roughly chop the bacon when it has cooled. Reserve about 2 tablespoons of the rendered bacon fat.

2 Fill a 6-quart pot with water. Bring it to a boil and add 2 tablespoons of salt. Add the pasta and cook until it's slightly firmer than al dente, 1 minute less than it says on the package, and drain, reserving 1 cup of cooking water.

3 While the water is coming to a boil, pour the reserved bacon fat and the olive oil into a large, heavy pot over medium-high heat. Add the garlic and cook for about 30 seconds. Add the tomatoes, bacon, 1 teaspoon of salt, a few grinds of black pepper, and stir. Let it cook for about 5 minutes, stirring occasionally.

4 Pour the pasta into the pot and stir. Add some of the cooking water if it looks dry, and taste for salt. Pour the pasta into a large serving dish, and place the egg yolks on top. Stir the yolks into the sauce right before serving.

Zero Ricotta Baked Ziti

SERVES 4 TO 6

Wine Pairings
RED: medium-bodied, juicy
Italian sangiovese
WHITE: smoky, savory
California chenin blanc

PASTA SHAPES: rigatoni,
penne, strozzapreti

SERVE WITH: dried red
chili flakes, grated Pecorino
Romano

Recipe Note

This recipe uses whole-milk,
"regular" mozzarella and
fresh mozzarella. The main
difference between the two
is the moisture content. I love
how fresh mozzarella melts
and browns on top, but it
would make the sauce slightly
too watery if I used it mixed in
with the ziti.

*I don't have anything against ricotta. But when I was growing up,
I ate BAD ricotta: soupy, grainy ricotta that tasted like salty water.
So I wanted a baked ziti with no ricotta. I wanted one baked with
loads of mozzarella and topped with even more mozzarella, because
it's hard (impossible?) to have too much mozzarella. So I made one,
and served it to lots of people who didn't miss the ricotta at all.*

1 medium white onion, quartered

3 cloves garlic, crushed

1 (28-ounce) can whole, peeled
San Marzano tomatoes, with
juices

Kosher salt

Freshly ground black pepper

4 tablespoons salted butter,
diced

1 pound ziti

8 ounces whole-milk mozzarella,
diced

2 cups freshly grated Pecorino
Romano

1 cup coarsely chopped fresh
basil, divided

8 ounces fresh mozzarella, sliced

½ cup panko breadcrumbs

2 tablespoons extra-virgin
olive oil

1 Preheat the oven to 375°F.

2 Grease the bottom of a 9 by 13-inch lasagne pan with butter or
cooking spray. Combine the onions, garlic, and tomatoes with juices in
the pan. Season with 1 teaspoon of salt and a few grinds of black pepper,
and dot the butter on top. Cook for 35 minutes, until caramelized.

3 While the sauce is cooking, fill a 6-quart pot with water, bring it to
a boil, and add 2 tablespoons of salt. Parboil the ziti by cooking it for
1 minute less than half of what it says on the package (for example, if it
says to cook for 12 to 14 minutes, then cook for 5 minutes), and drain.

4 Remove the sauce from the oven, pour it into a blender or food
processor, and purée until smooth.

5 Transfer the sauce and the ziti to a large mixing bowl and add the
diced mozzarella, pecorino, and half of the basil. Toss to combine, and
taste for salt, adding more if needed. Pour the pasta into the lasagne
pan. Top with the fresh mozzarella, sprinkle with the panko, and drizzle
with olive oil. Bake for 30 minutes, and then turn on the broiler. Place dish
about 4 inches from the broiler for 1 to 2 minutes, until the top begins to
brown. Sprinkle the remaining basil over the pasta before serving.

Whole-Wheat Thin Spaghetti with Zucchini and Onions

SERVES 4 TO 6

Wine Pairings
RED: medium-bodied, easy-drinking Montepulciano d'Abruzzo
WHITE: balanced, light Italian Soave

PASTA SHAPES: whole-wheat spaghetti, linguine, bucatini

SERVE WITH: grated Pecorino Romano, dried red chili flakes

I had the opportunity to learn how to make fresh pasta from the family behind my favorite brand of pasta, Rustichella d'Abruzzo, and it was spectacular. While I was in Abruzzo, they took me and about fifteen others from around the globe to their farms, mills, and factories, so we could understand not only how to make the pasta but where the grains come from. Rustichella has a line of pasta called PrimoGrano, in which they use a mix of heritage grains that are only grown in Abruzzo. It tastes like the pasta equivalent to freshly baked bread!

This recipe is my interpretation of a dish I had while I was in Abruzzo. It was a dish they served to us after we learned how to make traditional chitarra from Stefania Peduzzi, who owns Rustichella with her brother Gianluigi. The sauce was silky, brothy, and salty in the way only pork fat can make it. If you can't find PrimoGrano spaghetti, be sure to look for another high-quality brand of whole-wheat spaghetti (because honestly, most of them are not very good).

3 tablespoons unsalted butter

3 tablespoons extra-virgin olive oil, divided

1 large yellow onion, halved, and thinly sliced into half-moons

Kosher salt

2 medium zucchini, halved lengthwise and cut into thin half-moons

2 large carrots, halved lengthwise and cut into thin half-moons

3 cloves garlic, minced

1 cup chicken stock, preferably homemade

Freshly ground black pepper

1 pound whole-wheat thin spaghetti

6 ounces guanciale, diced

½ cup chopped fresh flat leaf parsley

Freshly grated Pecorino Romano, for serving

1   Melt the butter in a large sauté pan over medium heat, and add 2 tablespoons of the olive oil. Add the onions and 1 teaspoon of salt. Cook for 2 minutes, stirring often. Add the zucchini and carrots and continue sautéing for another 5 minutes. Push the vegetables to the sides of the pan, making a well. Add the garlic to the middle, and sauté for about 30 seconds. Add the stock and a few grinds of black pepper, and decrease the heat to medium-low. Let it cook for about 5 minutes, until the vegetables have softened.

2 While the sauce is cooking, fill a 6-quart pot with water, bring it to a boil, and add 2 tablespoons of salt. Add the pasta and stir. Cook until slightly firmer than al dente, 1 minute less than it says on the package, and drain, reserving 1 cup of cooking water. Pour the spaghetti back into the pot.

3 Place a small skillet over medium-high heat and add the remaining 1 tablespoon of olive oil. When it's hot, add the guanciale. Cook until the fat has rendered and the meat is slightly browned, about 6 minutes.

4 Pour the guanciale and the rendered fat over the pasta and set over low heat. Toss to fully coat, pour in the zucchini sauce, and stir again, adding a little of the cooking water if needed. Taste for salt and pepper, adding slowly if it needs more. Pour into a large serving dish and top with parsley and plenty of freshly grated cheese.

Gemelli with Blistered Tomatoes and Balsamic Butter

SERVES 4 TO 6

This is one of those recipes that takes so little time to prep you almost feel guilty serving it to a crowd—until you see their reaction when they try it. Who knew sheet-pan pasta could be a thing? If only you could boil the pasta on a sheet pan.

Look for "real" balsamic vinegar from Italy. Look on the label for D.O.P., which stands for Denominazione di Origine Protetta (Protected Designation of Origin). This is a guarantee that the product was made by farmers and artisans using traditional methods. It ranges in price, and usually the thicker it is, the more expensive it will be. Get one that's priced around $20 per bottle.

Wine Pairings
RED: bright, acidic California pinot noir
WHITE: fruity, bright French sauvignon blanc

PASTA SHAPES: casarecce, fusilli, linguine

SERVE WITH: dried red chili flakes, grated ricotta salata

Recipe Note
Ricotta salata is a Sicilian sheep's-milk cheese with a texture similar to feta. If you can't find it, use queso fresco or Pecorino Romano as a substitute.

If you use a thin, less expensive vinegar, heat it in a small saucepan with the butter to thicken it up a bit before mixing it with the tomatoes.

---

5 tablespoons unsalted butter, melted

2 tablespoons thick Italian balsamic vinegar

Kosher salt

2½ pounds cherry tomatoes or Early Girl tomatoes

3 cloves garlic, smashed

1 tablespoon extra-virgin olive oil, plus extra for drizzling

1 pound gemelli

½ cup finely grated ricotta salata or queso fresco

¼ cup chopped fresh flat leaf parsley

1 Preheat the oven to 400°F.

2 In a small bowl, whisk the butter, balsamic vinegar, and 1 teaspoon of salt.

3 Arrange the tomatoes and garlic on a baking sheet, and pour the balsamic butter and olive oil on top. Shake the tray to distribute evenly. Transfer to the oven and cook for 20 to 25 minutes, until the tomatoes start to break open.

4 While the tomatoes are cooking, fill a 6-quart pot with water, bring it to a boil, and add 2 tablespoons of salt. Add the pasta and stir. Cook until al dente, and drain.

5 When the tomatoes are done, remove them from the oven, pour the cooked pasta onto the baking sheet, and stir to coat with the tomatoes. Transfer to a large bowl and top with the grated cheese, parsley, and a drizzle of olive oil.

Tagliatelle with Ricotta Sauce and Fried Squash Blossoms

SERVES 4 TO 6

Wine Pairings
RED: light-bodied, fruity Italian lambrusco
WHITE: bright and bubbly French Champagne

PASTA SHAPES: fettuccine, spaghetti, linguine

SERVE WITH: dried red chili flakes, grated Parmigiano-Reggiano

I don't mean to go on and on about ricotta, but when I was growing up in New York, I had no idea that there was a world of good ricotta out there. But then I moved to California. I attended cheese shows, met cheese-makers, studied cheese, and ate as much cheese as humanly possible. I was opening a mac and cheese restaurant, and it was research! What surprised me the most was how delicious the ricotta I tasted was (and that it isn't pronounced "ree-goat," even though my family swears that it is).

This ricotta sauce is my dad's super-secret recipe, so don't tell him I shared it, or he may disown me. It works quite well with the watery ricotta, too, so if that's all you can find, then go for it.

1 pound whole-milk ricotta cheese
2 fresh large eggs
1 clove garlic, mashed into a paste
½ cup chopped fresh flat leaf parsley
1 cup finely grated Parmigiano-Reggiano
Kosher salt
Freshly ground black pepper
1 pound egg tagliatelle
1 pint cherry tomatoes, halved crosswise

FRIED SQUASH BLOSSOMS

1 cup all-purpose flour
1 (12-ounce) bottle of beer, or 12 ounces club soda
1 teaspoon kosher salt
Grapeseed oil, for frying
1 dozen squash blossoms, stamens removed

1 In a large mixing bowl, combine the ricotta, eggs, garlic, parsley, Parmigiano-Reggiano, 1 teaspoon of salt, and a few grinds of black pepper. Whisk until it looks silky and cohesive.

2 Fill a 6-quart pot with water. Bring it to a boil and add 2 tablespoons of salt. Add the pasta and stir. Cook until al dente (egg pasta gets mushy fast, so taste it frequently). Drain, reserving 1 cup of cooking water, and pour the pasta back into the pot.

3 Pour the ricotta sauce and half of the reserved water over the pasta and quickly toss with tongs. The cheese will begin to melt and form a rich sauce as it mixes with the eggs. Add more water if needed (this will depend on the consistency of your ricotta). Add the tomatoes, stir, and taste for salt, adding more if needed.

4 Serve immediately, with fried squash blossoms scattered on top.

FRIED SQUASH BLOSSOMS

To make the fried squash blossoms, gently whisk the flour, beer or club soda, and salt together in a mixing bowl. Heat about 2 inches of grapeseed oil in a saucepan over high heat. When the oil is hot (around 365°F), dip the blossoms into the batter and then directly into the oil. Fry for about 2 minutes, or until golden brown. Transfer to a plate lined with paper towels.

Farfalloni with Smoked Salmon and Creamy Corn Sauce

SERVES 4 TO 6

Wine Pairings
ROSE: fun, summery Spanish rosé Cava
WHITE: fresh, bright, unoaked French Chablis

PASTA SHAPES: garganelli, fusilli, gemelli

SERVE WITH: sliced jalapeño peppers, lemon wedges

Recipe Note
The salmon has a pretty strong flavor here. If you're not big on smoked salmon, just add a little on top instead of mixing it into the sauce.

Farfalle, the little bow tie pasta, has never been my favorite shape. It bothers me that the outside gets overcooked, while the bunched-up inside stays hard. But that's not the case with farfalloni, a larger bowtie. What a revelation! This shape is perfect for a crowd because it holds up really well in the sauce, and it looks super cute.

This sauce doesn't need any cheese, and I wouldn't bother having grated cheese on the table. I try to buy smoked salmon at the fish counter, where they let you sample different kinds before committing to one, since some are too sweet or too smoky. There are worse things in the world than tasting samples of smoked salmon! Choose one that's mild and tastes the freshest, but above all, make sure it's wild and not farmed.

Kosher salt

4 cups of fresh or frozen and thawed corn kernels

8 tablespoons salted butter

4 spring onions, green parts removed and finely chopped (or 3 shallots, finely chopped)

Freshly ground black pepper

1 cup heavy cream

1 pound farfalloni

5 ounces wild, cold-smoked salmon, cut into 2-inch pieces

1 tablespoon chopped fresh tarragon leaves

1 jalapeño pepper, sliced into thin rounds, for serving

1 If using fresh corn, fill a 6-quart pot with water, bring it to a boil, and add 1 tablespoon of salt. Add the corn and let it cook for 3 minutes. Drain, and set the corn aside. Skip this step if using frozen (thawed) corn. Refill the pot with water for the pasta, add 2 tablespoons of salt, and bring to a boil while you make the sauce.

2 Place the corn in a blender or food processor and purée it until it's relatively smooth (you'll still see some small bits, and that's OK).

3 Melt the butter in a large, heavy pot over medium heat. Add the spring onions or shallots and sauté for 2 minutes, until softened. Decrease the heat to low, and pour in the corn. Add 1 teaspoon of salt,

RECIPE CONTINUES ↓

**Farfalloni with
Smoked Salmon and
Creamy Corn Sauce,**
CONTINUED

a few grinds of pepper, and the cream, and stir. Let the sauce simmer for 10 minutes.

4 Place the pasta in the boiling water, and cook until slightly firmer than al dente, 1 minute less than it says on the package. Drain, reserving 1 cup of the cooking water.

5 Pour the pasta and half of the reserved cooking water into the pot with the corn sauce, and turn off the heat. Add half of the smoked salmon and the tarragon, and toss to combine. Add more of the remaining reserved cooking water if the sauce looks too thick. Taste for salt, adding more if needed. Pour into a big bowl and top with the remaining salmon and jalapeño slices. Serve immediately.

Stefania's Paccheri Fragola with Mozzarella and Crispy Basil

SERVES 4 TO 6

Wine Pairings

RED: medium-bodied, easy-drinking Spanish grenache
WHITE: dry, bubbly Italian prosecco

PASTA SHAPES: paccheri, calamarata, penne

SERVE WITH: dried red chili flakes, extra-virgin olive oil

Recipe Note

Colatura di alici is an Italian fish sauce made from anchovies, and you can find it at most Italian specialty stores or online. You can substitute Asian fish sauce in a pinch.

Stefania Peduzzi is the co-owner of the pasta company Rustichella d'Abruzzo, and let me tell you why I fell for her. She's a strikingly beautiful artist, mother, businesswoman, and world traveler, and she makes the best pasta I've ever had. When I was in Abruzzo, Stefania taught me how to make chitarra, a long pasta shape that's similar to spaghetti, but with square edges, because the dough is pushed through guitar strings.

Stefania and her family understand the importance of sharing meals with family and friends. They live it every day, when their extended family gathers for long lunches and leisurely dinners. Stefania makes this dish with paccherini alla fragola, a pasta made with strawberries! It's hard to find, so feel free to use regular paccheri if you can't find the fruity one.

Kosher salt

8 ounces buffalo mozzarella

1 tablespoon minced fresh thyme leaves

¾ cup whole milk, warmed

1 pound mezze paccheri or paccherini alla fragola

3 tablespoons extra-virgin olive oil, plus extra for frying and drizzling

1 tablespoon colatura di alici (Italian fish sauce) or Asian fish sauce

About 15 fresh basil leaves

1 Fill a 6-quart pot with water. Bring it to a boil and add 2 tablespoons of salt. While the water is coming to a boil, cut the mozzarella into small pieces and place it inside a blender with the thyme and milk. Blend together until smooth and creamy.

2 Cook the pasta until it's al dente, and drain. Put the pasta back into the pot and add the olive oil and fish sauce. Give it a stir to fully coat the pasta.

3 Coat the bottom of a small skillet with olive oil and place it over medium heat. When the oil is hot, gently add the basil leaves. Fry the leaves until they're crispy, about 3 minutes, and transfer to a plate lined with paper towels.

4 To serve, spoon some of the creamy cheese onto each plate and top with the pasta, a few basil leaves, and a drizzle of olive oil.

Trofie with Pesto Cream, Potatoes, and Green Beans

SERVES 4 TO 6

Wine Pairings
RED: big, fruity Italian Chianti
WHITE: bright, herbaceous California sauvignon blanc

PASTA SHAPES: strozzapreti, linguine, trenette

SERVE WITH: Lemon Breadcrumbs (page 160), fancy extra-virgin olive oil

The first time I had pasta and potatoes in the same dish was in Liguria, Italy, where they eat a surprising amount of potatoes (and where I also had a crazy delicious dish with anchovies and potatoes). If your gut is telling you, "Nah, pasta and potatoes are too starchy for me," you're in for a surprise. I love serving this dish for a crowd, because it's a real eye-opener. It's something people generally wouldn't order, but they're happy that they tried it. The recipe also adds cream to the pesto, which I don't usually make when I'm cooking just for my family, and I never order at restaurants, because it's often swimming in cream—but I do love what happens to the pesto when you add just a touch. It gets soft and silky, and feels luxurious.

Kosher salt
½ pound medium Yukon gold potatoes, thinly sliced
1 pound trofie

½ pound haricots verts
1 cup basic pesto (page 162)
½ cup heavy cream

1 Fill a 6-quart pot with water. Bring it to a boil and add 2 tablespoons of salt. Add the potatoes and let them cook for 10 minutes, until they're softened but still firm. Add the trofie, and when the pasta is 1 minute away from being al dente, throw in the green beans, and cook for 1 minute. Drain, reserving ½ cup of the cooking water.

2 Place the pasta, potatoes, and beans back into the pot over the lowest heat. Add the pesto and cream, and toss. If it doesn't look saucy enough, add a little of the cooking water and cook for 1 to 2 minutes, until hot. Taste for salt, adding more if needed. Pour the pasta into a large bowl, and serve immediately.

Grandma's Simple Tomato Salad with Buttery Crostini

SERVES 4 TO 6

Great-Grandma Fabrizio lived one town over when I was growing up. I spent Sundays at her house for dinner, but I also spent weekdays there—learning how to knit, having "coffee" with her girlfriends (the little old Italian ladies), and playing in the garden. In the summer, Grandma always had tons of tomatoes growing and more hot pepper plants than I could count. No matter what we were eating, there was always a small bowl of freshly minced hot peppers on the table. I didn't appreciate this until I was older, but now I especially love them on her simple tomato salad, with the crunch and heat of fresh hot peppers swirled with soft, sweet garden tomatoes— especially when you have a thick slice of fresh bread to dunk into the spicy tomato juices left on the plate. When I made this salad for Pasta Friday, my friend Lenny dropped a piece of bread into the big salad platter, let it soak, and came back for it a minute later. He was my hero that night!

1 medium red onion, halved and thinly sliced

3 pounds ripe, red tomatoes, quartered (I love using Early Girl or Jackpot tomatoes.)

½ cup coarsely chopped fresh flat leaf parsley

½ cup coarsely chopped fresh basil leaves

¾ cup extra-virgin olive oil

¼ cup red wine vinegar

1 teaspoon kosher salt

1–2 jalapeño or serrano peppers (depending on how spicy you want it), finely chopped or sliced

Flaky sea salt

BUTTERY CROSTINI

1 baguette, sliced in half lengthwise

1 clove garlic, mashed into a paste

3–4 tablespoons salted butter, melted

1 Soak the red onion slices in cold water for at least 10 minutes to tame their bite. While they're getting an ice bath, prepare the rest of the salad.

2 In a large bowl, combine the tomatoes, parsley, basil, olive oil, vinegar, and salt, and give it a good toss. Drain the onions, add them to the bowl, and toss again. Let the salad stand at room temperature for at least 30 minutes. Add the hot peppers right before serving so they don't lose their crunch. Taste for salt, and add flaky sea salt if needed.

BUTTERY CROSTINI

To make the buttery crostini, preheat the oven to 350°F. In a small bowl, whisk the garlic paste and butter. Use a spoon or pastry brush to spread the garlic butter all over both halves of the bread. Bake for 10 to 12 minutes, until just starting to brown. Cut into slices and serve next to the salad.

Cucumber Basil Salad with Anchovies and Croutons

SERVES 4 TO 6

I have a close friend named Bahareh (pronounced Baja Ray) who moved to the United States from Iran when she was twenty-four and barely spoke English. Fast-forward twenty years, and she owns her own business, runs a Persian school for kids, and is one of the best mamas I know. I love her for many reasons, not the least of which is that she introduced me to Persian cucumbers, which are by far the best tasting cucumbers! I give them about half an hour to soak up the salt and lemon juice before tossing them with the rest of this salad.

2 pounds Persian cucumbers, cut into ¼-inch thin rounds

1 cup fresh lemon juice

1½ teaspoons kosher salt

Freshly ground black pepper

1 head butter lettuce, torn into bite-sized pieces

2 cups Homemade Lemon Croutons (page 160)

1 cup coarsely chopped fresh basil

½ cup chopped pistachios

6 anchovy filets, coarsely chopped

Extra-virgin olive oil

Flaky sea salt

1   Place the cucumbers, lemon juice, kosher salt, and a few grinds of black pepper in a medium bowl, and toss to combine. Let stand at room temperature for about 30 minutes, then drain.

2   Meanwhile, place the lettuce, croutons, basil, pistachios, and anchovies in a large bowl and toss. When you're ready to serve, add the cucumbers and toss again. Dress lightly with about 2 to 3 tablespoons of your fancy olive oil and a sprinkle of flaky sea salt.

Classic Chopped Italian Salad

SERVES 4 TO 6

This was the salad I made for my first Pasta Friday. I chose this salad because it reminded me of the Italian restaurants in Queens, where I'd go with my family when I was growing up. They all had their own version of this salad, but always with salami, provolone, red onion, lots of vinegar, and always chopped.

My grandmother died a week before my first Pasta Friday dinner. When a Catholic living on Long Island passes away, it's tradition for the family of the deceased to host a lunch immediately following the burial, inviting everyone who came to the cemetery (including the weird people who show up at cemeteries just for a lunch invite). We hosted the big lunch at an Italian restaurant near her house, and of course, they served the classic Italian chopped salad.

½ cup thinly sliced red onion (about half a medium onion)

1 head romaine lettuce, chopped into 1-inch pieces

4 ounces Italian salami, thinly sliced into rounds and cut into quarters

4 ounces aged provolone (or Asiago), thinly sliced and cut into 1-inch pieces

1 cup cherry tomatoes, halved crosswise

1 cup black olives, like kalamata, pitted and halved

½ cup chopped fresh flat leaf parsley

About 10 whole pepperoncini, drained

GARLIC VINAIGRETTE

¼ cup red wine vinegar

1 clove garlic, mashed into a paste

1 tablespoon freshly squeezed lemon juice

1 teaspoon kosher salt

1 cup fruity olive oil

1 Soak the onion in cold water for at least 10 minutes, and drain. Place the lettuce, salami, provolone, red onion, tomatoes, olives, parsley, and pepperoncini in a large serving bowl.

2 To make the dressing, combine the vinegar, garlic, lemon juice, and salt in a small bowl. Slowly drizzle in the olive oil, whisking constantly to emulsify. Taste for salt, adding more if needed.

3 Slowly drizzle the dressing down the sides of the bowl, about 1 tablespoon at a time, gently tossing the salad as you go, until all of the ingredients are slightly wet (you'll have dressing left over). Serve immediately with the extra dressing on the side.

Butter Lettuce with Prosciutto, Peaches, and Burrata

SERVES 4 TO 6

I cook for crowds almost every week, and I try never to repeat a recipe, so I sometimes put together dishes I wouldn't normally make just for my family. Cooking for other people helps me branch out from my go-to flavor combos and think about what everyone will enjoy eating. This salad is an example. I don't usually enjoy stone fruit in salads, even though northern California has some of the sweetest stone fruit I have ever tasted. I really enjoy this salad, though, and not only because it has burrata (but maybe mostly because it has burrata).

1 head butter lettuce, chopped into bite-sized pieces (about 2 inches)

3 pounds ripe, slightly soft peaches, each one cut into 8 wedges (skin on)

4 ounces prosciutto, thinly sliced and cut into long strips

½ cup coarsely chopped mint leaves

8 ounces burrata, room temperature

About ¼ cup fruity, extra-virgin olive oil, plus extra for serving

2 teaspoons thick, syrupy balsamic vinegar

Flaky sea salt

1   You will need a large platter, approximately 11 by 16 inches, to assemble the salad.

2   Scatter the lettuce over the platter.

3   Scatter the peaches over the lettuce. Gather each slice of prosciutto into a loose ball, and place them around the peaches. Sprinkle the mint leaves all over the salad.

4   Tear the burrata into bite-sized pieces and spread evenly over the salad. Use a spoon to get any cream that spills out and drizzle that over, too! Drizzle the olive oil all over the salad, then the vinegar, and finally the salt. Don't toss before serving! Leave it as is, and serve with extra olive oil and flaky salt on the side.

FALL

The weather in Oakland doesn't cool down until mid-November, when we finally get to wear comfy sweaters, tall boots, and jean jackets. And yes, we even get to see a few leaves change color! Pasta Friday during the fall season means kids in Halloween costumes and thicker, creamier sauces, now that there's no longer a need to worry about looking good in beachside photos. The crowd grows in the fall, since vacations are over and everyone is settling into the new school year. Fall is also the season for new friends. The boys love to invite kids from their classes to Pasta Friday and involve them in our weekly tradition!

FALL PASTA

Duck Lasagne with Roasted Carrots 50

Orecchiette with Broccolini, Sausage, and Beans 54

Radiatore with Crispy Chicken, Carrots, and Sage 56

Filei with Wild Mushrooms, Lemon, and Garlic 59

Campanelle and Shrimp in a Rich Pink Cream Sauce 61

Cavatappi Fagioli with Toppings Bar 63

Cheesy Baked Cavatelli with Sausage and Herbs 66

Cacio e Pepe with Pici and Mushrooms 68

Sun-Dried Tomatoes, Sirloin, and Spinach with Chiocciole 70

Broken-Up Chicken Parm with Cestini 72

Mafaldine with Porcini and Eggs 75

Penne alla Vino 77

Crispy Cauliflower with Kale and Rotini 78

FALL SALADS

Avocado Bacon Salad with Salsa Verde 81

Fennel Salad with Grapes, Pine Nuts, and Aged Provolone 82

Crispy Potato Salad with Cranberries 83

Rainbow Carrots and Roasted White Beans with Bagna Cauda 84

Duck Lasagne with Roasted Carrots

SERVES 6 TO 8

Wine Pairings
RED: slightly sweet, fruity California pinot noir
WHITE: bright, acidic French Sancerre

PASTA SHAPES: only lasagna sheets!

SERVE WITH: crushed Calabrian chiles in oil, grated Pecorino Romano

It is absolutely okay to let other people host Pasta Friday! Having guests at your house every Friday, or even once a month, can quickly feel like a chore, and a stressful chore at that, and can take all of the enjoyment out of the tradition. So if friends ever suggest hosting a Pasta Friday at their house, take them up on it! Our friends Laura and Ara offered one week when I was especially drained and not in the mood to have twenty-five kids at my house, and I was SO grateful. And, Ara makes the most incredible bread in his backyard, wood-burning oven.

I made lasagne, because I could assemble it at home and bake it in their oven for a low-stress dinner. And I made this lasagne in particular, because it's decadent, comforting, and elegant, and so out of the ordinary. Fresh pasta sheets work best, but don't feel obligated to make them—just pick up fresh sheets from an Italian market or grocery store.

DUCK RAGÙ
1 whole duck (about 4 pounds), quartered
Kosher salt
Freshly ground black pepper
¼ cup extra-virgin olive oil
4 cloves garlic, minced
2 large carrots, peeled and diced
2 stalks celery, finely chopped
1 large white onion, finely chopped
1 tablespoon tomato paste
1½ cups dry white wine
1 (28-ounce) can whole, peeled San Marzano tomatoes, with juices
1 teaspoon chopped fresh marjoram

ROASTED CARROTS
5 large carrots, peeled and cut into ¼-inch rounds, about 3 cups
2 tablespoons extra-virgin olive oil
1 teaspoon freshly ground black pepper
½ teaspoon kosher salt

ASSEMBLY
Kosher salt
1 pound fresh lasagna sheets (homemade or store-bought; dried sheets work in a pinch)
Butter, for greasing
1½ cups freshly grated Pecorino Romano
1½ cups freshly grated Parmigiano-Reggiano
¼ cup chopped fresh flat leaf parsley

1 To make the ragù, season the duck quarters all over with salt and pepper.

2 Pour the olive oil into a large, heavy pan over medium-high heat. When the oil is hot, add the duck, and sear on all sides until some fat has rendered and the duck is browned, about 8 minutes. Transfer the duck to a plate and decrease the heat to medium.

3 Add the garlic, carrots, celery, and onions to the pan and cook for 5 minutes, scraping up any bits on the bottom. Add the tomato paste and cook for about 3 minutes, until caramelized. Return the duck to the pot. Add the wine ½ cup at a time, letting it cook until most of the wine has evaporated before the next addition, about 15 minutes total, stirring occasionally. Add the tomatoes and juices from the can, breaking apart the tomatoes with your hands as you add them to the pot. Add 1 teaspoon of salt and a few grinds of pepper, and when it starts to boil, decrease the heat to low, cover, and simmer for 1 hour.

4 To make the roasted carrots, preheat the oven to 400°F. Place the carrot slices on a baking sheet, add the oil, pepper, and salt, and toss to evenly coat. Roast the carrots for 15 minutes, until they just begin to brown. Remove the carrots from the oven and reduce the temperature to 350°F.

5 Remove the duck pieces from the sauce and let cool slightly. Discard the skin and remaining fat, and shred the meat from the bones (this is a bit of a pain). Return the meat to the sauce, stir in the marjoram, and simmer over low heat while you assemble the rest of the ingredients.

6 To assemble, fill a large pot with water and bring it to a boil. Add 2 tablespoons of salt. Cook the pasta sheets for only 20 seconds, drain, and quickly place the sheets in an ice bath to stop the cooking process. Drain them again.

RECIPE CONTINUES ↓

7 Grease a 9 by 13-inch lasagne pan with butter. In a large bowl, mix the two cheeses together.

8 Spread a thin layer of the duck ragù on the bottom of the pan, and cover with a layer of pasta. Spread another layer of ragù, followed by a thin layer of carrots and a layer of cheese. Repeat with a layer of pasta, ragù, carrots, and cheese, and repeat the layers until the pan is full (you'll have about five layers). Finish with a layer of sauce and a final layer of cheese (no carrots). Don't cut the excess pasta around the edges as you're layering. Fold them inward, like piecrust, to create a ruffled top that's crispy and delicious!

9 Bake for 35 minutes, lightly covered with aluminum foil. Remove the foil and cook for an additional 10 to 15 minutes, until the top is golden brown and bubbly. Let stand for about 10 minutes before cutting. Sprinkle the parsley on top. Cut into squares and serve.

Orecchiette with Broccolini, Sausage, and Beans

SERVES 4 TO 6

Wine Pairings

RED: acidic, bright French gamay

WHITE: unoaked, crisp French Chardonnay

PASTA SHAPES: cavatelli, gnocchi, strozzapreti

SERVE WITH: Lemon Breadcrumbs (page 160), dried red chili flakes

---

Recipe Note

If you're using dried beans, soak them overnight and drain. Place them in a large pot and cover with water by about 2 inches. Add some olive oil, black pepper, and bay leaves, and simmer for about 1 hour, until tender. Add a little salt, and drain.

Another trick I learned from cooking for a crowd is it's much easier to make a big pot of sauce than it is to combine separate ingredients into a cohesive dish. It's still doable with separate ingredients, though, and using a sheet pan and the oven helps. I use my oven for things like cooking sausage and roasting beans, and once you master it, sheet-pan Pasta Fridays are no hassle at all. While you can easily make this dish on the stove, I'll tell you how to put it together in your oven.

Dried cannellini beans that have been soaked overnight have the best texture, so if you have time, I recommend using them. However, it's rare that I (or most people I know) have that extra time, so don't feel bad about using canned beans. Look for organic beans that don't have anything other than salt added, and if you can find them, buy the ones that come in a box (I like the 365 brand from Whole Foods).

1½ pounds mild or spicy Italian sausage, casing removed, crumbled

Extra-virgin olive oil

2 cans cannellini beans, drained and rinsed

1 pound broccolini, cut into 2-inch pieces

Kosher salt

Freshly ground black pepper

1 pound orecchiette

5 tablespoons unsalted butter

¾ cup finely grated Parmigiano-Reggiano

1 teaspoon minced fresh rosemary

1 Preheat the oven to 400°F.

2 Dry the sausage with paper towels, and spread it on a baking sheet. Drizzle with 1 tablespoon of olive oil. Bake for 10 minutes without stirring, flip, and cook for about 5 minutes more, or until browned.

3 Gently dry the beans with paper towels. Place the beans and broccolini in a large bowl and add 2 tablespoons of olive oil, 1 teaspoon of salt, and a few grinds of pepper. Toss to coat, then spread the beans and broccolini on a baking sheet. Cook in the oven for 15 minutes.

4 Meanwhile, fill a 6-quart pot with water. Bring it to a boil and add 2 tablespoons of salt. Cook the pasta until al dente and drain, reserving 1 cup of cooking water. Pour the pasta back into the pot.

5 Melt the butter in a small saucepan over medium-low heat. Swirl it around as it begins to foam. When the foaming subsides, cook for 1 minute longer, until it turns golden brown, without burning. Pour the browned butter over the pasta and add the cheese, rosemary, and ½ cup of the cooking water, and stir to combine.

6 Add the sausage and any accumulated juices to the pasta. Add the beans and broccolini, and toss it all together. Add the rest of the cooking water if it looks dry. Taste for salt, and drizzle your fancy olive oil on top.

Radiatore with Crispy Chicken, Carrots, and Sage

SERVES 6 TO 8

Wine Pairings
RED: bright, fruity French Côtes du Rhône
WHITE: grassy and apple-y French Chablis

PASTA SHAPES: rotini, campanelle, gemelli

SERVE WITH: grated Pecorino Romano, crushed Calabrian chiles in oil

Coming up with new recipes for Pasta Friday is not always easy. Sometimes I use an old family recipe, or a tried-and-true pasta dish, or something new and exciting that popped into my head while I was taking a shower. Other times, I am blocked, panicked even, because for the life of me, I can't think of a single thing to cook for all those people who are coming to dinner. The inspiration for this dish came to me one week when I was out of ideas, and Luca (luckily?) caught a cold. While I was making him chicken soup, I thought of this recipe.

Roast a chicken if you have time, but don't feel bad about picking up an organic, roasted chicken from the butcher or supermarket. Also, if you want to replace your Thanksgiving turkey with a pasta dish, this one is it. One bite and I guarantee no one will even miss it.

1 (3 to 4-pound) whole, roasted chicken, juices reserved
¼ cup extra-virgin olive oil
6 tablespoons salted butter
1 pound medium carrots, peeled and thinly sliced into rounds
4 shallots, thinly sliced
Kosher salt
1 teaspoon ground Aleppo pepper

Freshly ground black pepper
6 sage leaves, chopped
¼ cup pine nuts, lightly toasted
1 lemon, quartered, seeds removed
1 pound radiatore
½ cup panko breadcrumbs, lightly toasted

1 Preheat the oven to 375°F.

2 Carefully remove the skin from the roasted chicken and spread it out on a baking sheet lined with parchment paper. Place the chicken skin in the oven and cook for about 10 minutes, until it gets crispy. Remove from the oven, and when it cools, crumble it into small pieces and place in a small bowl.

3 While the skin is in the oven, pull the meat from the chicken bones and shred it using a fork. Place the meat in a bowl and discard the bones. Reserve the juices.

RECIPE CONTINUES ↓

4 Switch your oven to broil. Spread the chicken meat out on a baking sheet, and drizzle on the olive oil. Place meat about 4 inches from the broiler and cook for about 2 minutes, until it gets a browned and crispy edge. Stir it around and broil for another 2 minutes. Remove it from the broiler and set aside.

5 Melt the butter in a large, heavy pot over medium-high heat. Add the carrots, shallots, and 1 teaspoon of salt, and sauté for about 6 minutes, until softened. Add a few grinds of black pepper and the Aleppo, and cook for 1 minute more. Add the sage and pine nuts, squeeze the lemons into the pot, then throw the lemon quarters in, too. Pour the chicken into the pot and toss. Decrease the heat to low and let it simmer while the pasta is cooking.

6 Fill a 6-quart pot with water. Bring it to a boil and add 2 tablespoons of salt. Add the radiatore and stir. Cook until slightly firmer than al dente, 1 minute less than it says on the package, and drain, reserving ½ cup of cooking water.

7 Pour the pasta into the pot with the chicken. Add the reserved chicken juices and the panko, and toss. Taste for salt, adding more if needed. Add a little of the reserved cooking water if it looks too dry. Top with the crispy chicken skin and a drizzle of olive oil, and serve family-style.

Filei with Wild Mushrooms, Lemon, and Garlic

SERVES 4 TO 6

Wine Pairings
RED: ripe, earthy Spanish Rioja
WHITE: oaky, silky California chardonnay

PASTA SHAPES: strozzapreti, trofie, tagliatelle

SERVE WITH: Crispy, Spicy Prosciutto (page 161), grated Grana Padano

Few ingredients are as divisive as mushrooms (maybe beets come close). People often ask me what I do if guests don't like the recipe I'm preparing, and my answer is nothing. Guests are welcome to bring their own food if they have dietary restrictions, or they can decide not to eat what I made, but what happens most often is people try something they didn't think they liked and end up loving it—like mushrooms. I never change the menu, though, based on guest preferences. That can lead me down a slippery slope.

It's not easy making wild mushrooms for a big group. Mushrooms are finicky, and if you overcrowd the pan, they become soggy and won't brown. This recipe is best with a mix of wild mushrooms, but using all shiitakes will also work.

1½ pounds assorted wild mushrooms (preferably chanterelle, shiitake, oyster, and pioppini)

5 tablespoons salted butter

1 tablespoon Roasted Garlic (page 20)

Kosher salt

½ cup fresh lemon juice

2 teaspoons finely grated lemon zest

1 pound filei pasta

8 ounces whole-milk mozzarella, diced

½ cup coarsely chopped fresh flat leaf parsley

½ cup coarsely chopped fresh mint

¼ cup pine nuts, lightly toasted

Freshly ground black pepper

1   Gently brush any dirt from the mushrooms with a paper towel. Trim the stems, and slice the mushrooms ½ inch thick.

2   Melt the butter in a large sauté pan over medium heat. Add the roasted garlic and gently stir to blend with the butter. Add the mushrooms and 1 teaspoon of salt. If you can't comfortably fit the mushrooms in a single layer, work in batches so they don't steam. Cook for about 8 minutes, stirring every minute or so, until they are nicely browned and crisp. Add the lemon juice and zest, stir, and turn off the heat.

RECIPE CONTINUES ↓

3 While the mushrooms are cooking, fill a 6-quart pot with water and bring it to a boil. Add 2 tablespoons of salt, then add the pasta and stir. When the pasta is slightly firmer than al dente, 1 minute less than it says on the package, drain and reserve 1 cup cooking water. Pour the pasta back into the pot and place over low heat.

4 Pour the mushroom sauce over the pasta. Add the mozzarella, parsley, mint, pine nuts, a few grinds of black pepper, and half of the reserved cooking water. Give it a good toss, and taste for salt, adding more if needed. Add more of the remaining reserved cooking water, a little at a time, if it looks too dry. Pour into a serving dish and serve family-style.

Campanelle and Shrimp in a Rich Pink Cream Sauce

SERVES 6 TO 8

Wine Pairings
RED: tart Italian Chianti
WHITE: subtle, slightly savory Italian Soave

PASTA SHAPES: rigatoni, penne, ziti

SERVE WITH: Crispy, Spicy Prosciutto (page 161), Green Garlic Bread (page 162)

Some Pasta Friday dinners are burned deeply into my brain, and I can easily tell you who was there, what we talked about, and which child dripped melted Popsicle juice all over my carpet. The night I served this was one of those nights. I think it was because the sauce turned out better than I expected—I was testing out this dish for the first time, and I was slightly worried it was perhaps too smoky, spicy, or briny.

After I served it, Trevor, a lawyer and Pasta Friday regular, kept asking me for the recipe, and a few guests said it was the best Pasta Friday dinner yet. So crisis averted. The sauce is intense in the best way possible, with the sun-dried tomatoes and anchovies, while the shrimp mellows it out a bit. I don't bother putting cheese out with this one!

1 (28-ounce) can whole, peeled San Marzano tomatoes, with juices

1 (14.5-ounce) can whole, peeled San Marzano tomatoes, with juices

1 large white onion, coarsely chopped

4 cloves garlic

5 tablespoons extra-virgin olive oil, divided

Kosher salt

1½ pounds medium shrimp, peeled and deveined, tails removed

½ cup fresh lemon juice

1½ teaspoons smoked sweet paprika

Freshly ground black pepper

8 ounces oil-packed sun-dried tomatoes, drained

4 tablespoons unsalted butter

1 tablespoon anchovy paste, or 3 anchovy filets, minced

¾ cup heavy cream

1 pound campanelle

1 Preheat the oven to 350°F.

2 Combine the whole tomatoes from the cans (reserve the juice for later) with the onions and garlic in a 9 by 13-inch lasagne pan. Drizzle on 4 tablespoons of the olive oil and season with 1 teaspoon of salt. Cook for 1 hour.

3 Toss the shrimp, the remaining 1 tablespoon of olive oil, lemon juice, smoked paprika, ½ teaspoon of salt, and a few grinds of pepper in a large bowl, and let marinate while the sauce is cooking.

RECIPE CONTINUES ↓

4 Arrange the shrimp in a single layer on a baking sheet and place in the oven. Cook for about 4 minutes, just until they turn pink and not any longer. Remove them from the oven and place in a bowl (don't keep them on the hot baking sheet, as they'll overcook).

5 In the bowl of a food processor or blender, combine the cooked tomato sauce and the sun-dried tomatoes, and purée until smooth, working in batches if necessary.

6 Melt the butter in a large, heavy pot over medium heat. Add the anchovy paste and stir until dissolved.

7 Add the reserved tomato juice from the cans, the puréed sauce, and the cream, and stir. Taste for salt. Keep at a low simmer, stirring every few minutes.

8 Fill a 6-quart pot with water. Bring it to a boil and add 2 tablespoons of salt. Add the campanelle and stir. Cook until the pasta is slightly firmer than al dente, 1 minute less than it says on the package, then drain. Pour the pasta into the pot with the sauce. Add the shrimp and stir to combine. Taste for salt, adding more if needed, and cook until the pasta is done, about 2 minutes. Transfer to a large bowl and serve immediately.

Cavatappi Fagioli with Toppings Bar

SERVES 6 TO 8

Wine Pairings
RED: easy-drinking, fruity
California grenache
WHITE: light-bodied, full-
flavored Italian ribolla gialla

PASTA SHAPES: fusilli, broken
spaghetti, cestini

SERVE WITH: all the toppings!

A fun way to host a party is to make a big pot of soup and let the guests add their own toppings. The first time I came across this presentation was in Colombia, visiting my husband Alejandro's family. His aunt made traditional ajiaco soup, a chicken soup with potatoes, and served it surrounded by bowls of capers, crema, tortilla strips, cheese, and hot peppers, so we could pick and choose how we wanted to dress up the soup.

This soup has the same inspiration, with a traditional Italian pasta fagioli soup receiving the Colombian treatment. It's also fun to see what toppings your friends choose. Every bowl is a completely different dish!

SOUP

1 cup dried cannellini beans, soaked overnight

1 cup dried pinto beans, soaked overnight

Kosher salt

Freshly ground black pepper

1 tablespoon dried oregano

1 Parmigiano-Reggiano rind

2 tablespoons extra-virgin olive oil

8 ounces pancetta, diced

1 medium yellow onion, finely chopped

4 large carrots, peeled and finely chopped

3 stalks celery, finely chopped

4 cloves garlic, minced

1 pound mild Italian sausage, casing removed, crumbled

1 (14.5-ounce) can whole, peeled San Marzano tomatoes, with juices

2 cups good-quality chicken stock, preferably homemade

1 pound cavatappi

TOPPINGS (PICK AND CHOOSE, OR ADD YOUR OWN!)

Fried Capers (page 161)

2 cups shaved Parmigiano-Reggiano

2 ripe tomatoes, coarsely chopped

1 cup coarsely chopped celery leaves

2 jalapeño peppers, minced

1 cup Garlic Breadcrumbs (page 160)

1 avocado, diced

1 cup coarsely chopped wild arugula

I To prepare the soup, place the beans in a medium pot with 2½ quarts of water, 1 tablespoon of salt, 1 tablespoon of black pepper, oregano, and the Parmigiano-Reggiano rind. Bring to a boil, cover the pot, and simmer over low heat for about 1½ hours, or until the beans are tender. Discard the rind.

RECIPE CONTINUES ↓

2 While the beans are cooking, heat the olive oil in a large, heavy pot over medium-high heat. Add the pancetta and cook until browned, about 5 or 6 minutes. Remove with a slotted spoon and place on a plate lined with paper towels. Add the onions, carrots, and celery, and cook until softened, about 6 minutes. Add the garlic and cook for 1 minute more. Add the sausage and cook for about 8 minutes, or until it's no longer pink. Decrease heat to medium, and add the tomatoes and juices from the can, breaking them apart with your hands as you go. Return the pancetta to the pot and cook for 5 minutes.

3 Add the beans and their liquid and the chicken stock to the pot. Cook for 10 minutes, then add the pasta and cook until al dente.

4 Serve from the pot with a ladle, and have all the toppings close by in small bowls.

Cheesy Baked Cavatelli with Sausage and Herbs

SERVES 4 TO 6

Wine Pairings
RED: earthy, full-bodied Argentinian Malbec
WHITE: crisp, clean California pinot gris

PASTA SHAPES: radiatore, strozzapreti, penne

SERVE WITH: dried red chili flakes, grated Parmigiano-Reggiano

Having loads of kids at your house every week is taxing, to put it mildly. One week, a few six-year-old girls locked themselves in the bathroom and couldn't get out because they jammed the lock. Another week, I found a melted, red Popsicle under the rug. Don't get me started on the week the kids stuffed an obscene amount of bread and butter down the bathroom drain. But the "Pasta Friday Kids," as they call themselves, have formed their own bonds and their own community—and it's adorable.

It's great to have a baked pasta that you can prepare the night before serving, so you can pay more attention to all of the ways these adorable kids are ruining your house.

3 tablespoons extra-virgin olive oil, plus extra for drizzling

1 pound spicy or mild Italian sausage, casing removed, crumbled

Kosher salt

1 pound cavatelli

12 ounces fresh mozzarella, diced

¾ cup whole milk

1 tablespoon minced fresh oregano

1 tablespoon minced fresh sage

Freshly ground black pepper

3 Roma or San Marzano tomatoes, sliced lengthwise

¾ cup breadcrumbs

3 tablespoons unsalted butter, diced

1 Preheat the oven to 375°F.

2 Heat the olive oil in a large sauté pan over medium-high heat. Add the sausage, breaking up any big pieces with a wooden spoon, and cook, without stirring, for 5 minutes. Stir and cook for another 5 minutes, until the sausage browns and crisps and is fully cooked. Place the sausage and juices in a large mixing bowl.

3 While the sausage is cooking, fill a 6-quart pot with water, bring it to a boil, and add 2 tablespoons of salt. Add the cavatelli and stir. Parboil the pasta by cooking it for 1 minute less than half of the cooking time listed on the package. For example, if the package says to cook for 12 to 14 minutes, cook it for 5 minutes. Drain and add it to the bowl with the sausage.

4 Add the mozzarella, milk, oregano, sage, 1 teaspoon of salt, and a few grinds of pepper to the bowl, and stir to fully combine. Pour into a 9 by 13-inch lasagne pan, without smoothing, to allow some of the cavatelli to protrude and get crispy.

5 Arrange the tomato slices on top in a single layer, and generously sprinkle with the breadcrumbs. Dot the butter on top of the breadcrumbs.

6 Bake for 35 to 45 minutes, until the top is golden brown. Drizzle with olive oil before serving.

Cacio e Pepe with Pici and Mushrooms

SERVES 4 TO 6

I held off from making cacio e pepe for Pasta Friday for a long time, because everyone knows that making cacio e pepe for a crowd is crazy talk. It gets clumpy in the blink of an eye, but I think I pulled it off. The trick was to make it in batches. Instead of draining the pasta water, use tongs to pick up and move the pici directly into the sauce, so you can keep the water boiling for the next batch.

I made three batches for my guests, and the third batch was best. The starch in the cooking water created a richer cheese sauce. You can fake it by adding cheese rinds to the water with the pasta.

4 tablespoons unsalted butter

1 pound shiitake mushrooms, stemmed and halved lengthwise

Kosher salt

1 pound pici

2½ to 3 cups finely grated Pecorino Romano

2 tablespoons coarsely ground black pepper or peppercorns crushed with a mortar and pestle

¼ cup heavy cream, warmed (optional)

1 Preheat the oven to 250°F. Place an ovenproof serving bowl in the oven to stay warm.

2 Melt the butter in a medium skillet over medium-high heat. Add the mushrooms and a pinch of salt, and sauté for 8 minutes, until softened and beginning to crisp.

3 Fill a 6-quart pot with water. Bring it to a boil and add 2 tablespoons of salt. Add the pasta, and cook until slightly firmer than al dente, 1 minute less than it says on the package.

4 Remove the serving bowl from the oven, and use tongs to transfer the pasta into the warm bowl (keep the heat on under the water). Add the mushrooms to the pasta and toss to combine.

5 Place the cheese and pepper in a medium mixing bowl. Whisk in 1½ cups of the pasta cooking water until it forms a paste. If the cheese looks too clumpy, add some heavy cream, a little at a time. Pour the cheese sauce over the pasta and quickly toss, slowly adding another ½ cup of cooking water to loosen the sauce to your desired consistency. Serve immediately.

Sun-Dried Tomatoes, Sirloin, and Spinach with Chiocciole

SERVES 4 TO 6

I know some people don't like sun-dried tomatoes. I want to make it abundantly clear that this recipe is not for those people. It's for the rest of us, who crave the salty, chewy, meatiness sun-dried tomatoes add to any dish. When you find tender ones that are not packed in oil, those are the best (although I only see them at farmers' markets). When you buy them packed in oil, go for the Italian brands, and make sure they don't have any herbs or other flavors added. Loose or oil-packed tomatoes work well in this recipe, but the loose ones maintain a pleasantly chewy texture.

¼ cup extra-virgin olive oil, plus extra for drizzling

1 pound ground beef sirloin (Ask the butcher to grind it for you.)

Kosher salt

Freshly ground black pepper

1 medium yellow onion, diced

12 ounces sun-dried tomatoes, drained if oil-packed, chopped

1½ teaspoons finely chopped fresh rosemary

1 cup dry red wine, like merlot

10 ounces spinach, whole leaves with stems

1 pound chiocciole

¾ cup finely grated Grana Padano

¼ cup coarsely chopped fresh flat leaf parsley

1   Heat the olive oil in a large, heavy pot over medium-high heat. Place the meat in the pot and break apart with a wooden spoon. Season with 1 teaspoon of salt and a few grinds of black pepper. Let it cook without stirring for 4 minutes. Flip it over and cook for another 3 to 4 minutes, without stirring, until crispy and no longer pink when broken apart. Transfer with a slotted spoon to a bowl.

2   Add the onions to the same pot and sauté for 3 minutes, until softened. Add the sun-dried tomatoes, rosemary, and 1 teaspoon of salt, and cook for another 5 minutes, until the onions begin to brown. Add the wine and cook until it reduces by half, about 10 minutes. Add the meat to the sauce and decrease the heat to low. Stir the spinach into the sauce.

3 Meanwhile, fill a 6-quart pot with water. Bring it to a boil and add 2 tablespoons of salt. Add the pasta, and cook until slightly firmer than al dente, 1 minute less than what it says on the package, then drain, reserving 1 cup of cooking water.

4 Add the pasta to the pot with the sauce, along with half of the cooking water, the cheese, and the parsley. Toss well and cook for 2 minutes more, adding more of the cooking water if it looks too dry. Pour into a large serving dish and drizzle with some olive oil before serving.

Broken-Up Chicken Parm with Cestini

SERVES 6 TO 8

Wine Pairings
RED: light-bodied, structured Italian barbera
WHITE: dry, crisp Italian pinot grigio

PASTA SHAPES: campanelle, casarecce, torchio

SERVE WITH: grated Parmigiano-Reggiano, dried red chili flakes

Recipe Note
I ask the butcher to pound the chicken for me, because it's messy and it's a pain. If you're doing it yourself, buy the thinnest cutlets you can find and pound them on a cutting board with an empty wine bottle or a pestle.

One important lesson I learned early in my Pasta Friday journey: you have to set limits. I wasn't necessarily good at setting any kind of limits in my life. I had (and maybe still have) a hard time saying no. Whether it's because I'm afraid of missing out on something, or I don't want to make someone feel bad, I don't like to say no—except when it comes to Pasta Friday.

When I first started these dinners, I rarely put a cap on the RSVP list. I let the guest list grow and just made more food to accommodate all the people who wanted to come. Until, that is, the week I made chicken parm. I had sixty people at my house. Sixty. I was stressed because the sauce didn't taste right, the kids were running circles around the kitchen, and I was worried I wouldn't have enough food. But mainly the stress was stemming from the sheer number of people crowded around me! So, lesson learned: don't be afraid to say no.

2 (28-ounce) cans whole, peeled San Marzano tomatoes, with juices
3 tablespoons extra-virgin olive oil, plus extra for frying
1 large white onion, finely chopped
3 cloves garlic, finely chopped
1 teaspoon dried oregano
Kosher salt

Freshly ground black pepper
1½ pounds boneless, skinless chicken breasts, pounded thin, about ¼ inch
2 eggs, beaten
2 cups panko breadcrumbs
1 pound cestini pasta
1 pound fresh mozzarella, diced

1 In a blender or food processor, purée the tomatoes from the cans until smooth, reserving the juices for later.

2 Heat 3 tablespoons of olive oil in a large, heavy pot over medium heat. Add the onions and cook for 4 minutes, until softened, stirring occasionally. Add the garlic and cook for 1 minute more. Add the puréed tomatoes and the juices from just one of the cans. Save the juices from the other can for another use. Add oregano, 1 teaspoon of salt, and a few grinds of black pepper. When the sauce begins to boil, decrease the heat to low and simmer, uncovered, while you prepare the rest of the dish.

3 Season the chicken on all sides with salt and pepper. Have the bowl with the beaten eggs close by, and a dish with the panko. Dip a cutlet into the eggs to completely soak, and lift, letting the excess egg drip back into the bowl. Dredge the cutlet in the panko, covering it completely, and place it on a clean plate. Repeat with the remaining cutlets.

4 Pour olive oil into a large skillet to a depth of ¼ inch. Heat the oil until just before smoking, about 360°F. Place the cutlets in the pan, without overcrowding, and fry for 3 minutes. Flip over and cook for another 2 or 3 minutes, until golden brown and cooked through. Transfer the cutlets to a plate lined with paper towels to drain.

5 Bring a 6-quart pot of water to a boil and add 2 tablespoons of salt. Add the pasta to the boiling water, and cook until it's slightly firmer than al dente, 1 minute less than it says on the package. Drain and pour the pasta into the pot with the sauce to finish cooking, about 2 minutes more. Transfer to a large, deep bowl.

6 Serve the pasta, cutlets, and mozzarella in separate dishes, and let your guests fill their plates with a little (or a lot) from each one. I always suggest putting the mozzarella onto your plate first, followed by the pasta, and then the chicken, so the cheese can melt! Serve with olive oil and grated Parmigiano-Reggiano.

Mafaldine with Porcini and Eggs

SERVES 4 TO 6

Wine Pairings
RED: medium-bodied, dry Italian Enfer d'Arvier or sangiovese
WHITE: balanced, crisp French Chardonnay

PASTA SHAPES: fettuccine, pappardelle, tagliatelle

SERVE WITH: grated Parmigiano-Reggiano, dried red chili flakes

I ate a version of this dish on my honeymoon, in a small town in the Aosta Valley, which is right on the border of Italy and France. It was late, and the only restaurant in the town happened to be closed for a family party. Luckily they let us crash their celebration, but we were even luckier to be served a five-course meal, which was the best meal of our trip. It included this pasta. It also included the fifty-something-year-old birthday boy strutting around the restaurant in his boxer shorts (never did I wish so much that I understood Italian!).

I could not wait to recreate this dish for Pasta Friday. Be sure to serve it in a big dish, with the egg yolks still intact. Right before people dig in, break apart the yolks and swirl them into the sauce.

2 ounces dried, whole porcini mushrooms
Kosher salt
4 ripe plum tomatoes
3 tablespoons unsalted butter
1 tablespoon extra-virgin olive oil, plus extra for drizzling
2 shallots, finely chopped
Freshly ground black pepper

1 pound mafaldine
1 cup finely grated fontina d'Aosta cheese (regular fontina will work in a pinch)
½ cup chopped fresh flat leaf parsley
1 teaspoon minced fresh thyme leaves
4–5 fresh egg yolks

1 Place the mushrooms in a small bowl, cover with hot water, and soak for 20 minutes. Drain, reserving the liquid, and coarsely chop the mushrooms.

2 Meanwhile, fill a 6-quart pot with water, bring to a boil, and add 2 tablespoons of salt.

3 Halve the tomatoes crosswise, and squeeze or spoon out the seeds and juice into a bowl. Coarsely chop the tomato flesh, and save the juice and seeds for another use.

4 Melt the butter in a large sauté pan over medium-high heat and add the olive oil and shallots. Cook for 4 minutes, until softened, stirring occasionally. Add the mushrooms, ½ teaspoon of salt, and a few grinds of black pepper, and cook for 2 minutes more. Add ¼ to ½ cup of the mushroom liquid and the tomatoes, cook for 1 minute, and turn off the heat.

RECIPE CONTINUES ↓

5 Add the pasta to the boiling water, and cook until slightly firmer than al dente, 1 minute less than what it says on the package. Using tongs, transfer the pasta directly into the pan with the sauce and put the heat on low. Add the cheese, parsley, thyme, and ½ cup of the pasta cooking water, and quickly toss to melt the cheese. Add more of the cooking water if it looks too thick. Taste for salt.

6 Pour the pasta into a serving dish, and arrange the egg yolks on top. Drizzle with some fancy olive oil and a pinch of salt on each yolk. Mix yolks into the sauce before serving.

Penne Alla Vino

SERVES 4 TO 6

Wine Pairings
RED: lightly acidic, spicy Italian Chianti
WHITE: citrusy California sauvignon blanc

PASTA SHAPES: rigatoni, pasta al ceppo, campanelle

SERVE WITH: Crispy, Spicy Prosciutto (page 161), grated Parmigiano-Reggiano

Does the world need another Penne alla Vodka recipe? Yes, it does, except with wine instead of vodka! This play on vodka sauce is smoky and spicy and still as nostalgic and comforting as the original. I don't add vodka to it, because, to me, it doesn't add much flavor—plus I never have any in the house. I do, though, always have red wine on hand, and I love the complexity it gives the sauce.

3 tablespoons salted butter
2 tablespoons extra-virgin olive oil
1 large white onion, finely chopped
Kosher salt
2 teaspoons smoked sweet paprika
2 cloves garlic, minced

½ cup dry, earthy red wine, like merlot
1 (28-ounce) can whole, peeled San Marzano tomatoes
Freshly ground black pepper
¾ cup heavy cream
¾ cup finely grated Parmigiano-Reggiano
1 pound penne

1 Heat the butter and olive oil in a large, heavy pot over medium heat. When the butter melts, add the onions and 1 teaspoon of salt, and cook for about 10 minutes, until they soften and begin to caramelize. Add the smoked sweet paprika and cook for 1 minute, then add the garlic and sauté for about 30 seconds. Add the wine and simmer for 8 to 10 minutes, until it reduces by half.

2 Add the tomatoes from the can (don't add the juice yet), breaking them apart with your hands before they hit the pot. Cook the tomatoes, without stirring, for 5 minutes, then add the remaining tomato juice and a few grinds of pepper, and decrease the heat to low.

3 Fill a 6-quart pot with water. Bring it to a boil and add 2 tablespoons of salt.

4 Meanwhile, heat the heavy cream in a small saucepan. When it's hot but not boiling, whisk in the Parmigiano-Reggiano until the cheese melts. Stir the cheese sauce into the tomato sauce and simmer over low heat while the pasta is cooking.

5 Add the pasta to the boiling water and stir. Cook until slightly firmer than al dente, 1 minute less than it says on the package, and drain. Add the pasta to the sauce to finish cooking, about 2 minutes more. Serve it family-style right from the pot!

Crispy Cauliflower with Kale and Rotini

SERVES 4 TO 6

Wine Pairings
RED: Spanish Rioja
WHITE: Spanish Cava

PASTA SHAPES: penne, gemelli, campanelle

SERVE WITH: grated Pecorino Romano, Fried Capers (page 161)

Have you guys met Alejandro? We've been married a long time, and I love him very much, but he's a slightly picky eater. I once asked him to pick up cauliflower at the store, and he came home with an artichoke. I won't tell you what happened when I asked for Romanesco.

Cauliflower is not Alejandro's favorite, but even he likes it pan-roasted and crispy, perhaps because it absorbs the deliciousness from everything else that's in the pan, or perhaps because he doesn't realize he's eating cauliflower.

Kosher salt

½ cup extra-virgin olive oil, divided

1 large head cauliflower, any color, cored and finely chopped

1 pound rotini

¾ cup coarsely chopped walnuts

3 cloves garlic, minced

2 teaspoons grated lemon zest

1 teaspoon dried red chili flakes

2 large bunches (about 1 pound) Tuscan kale, stems trimmed, ribs and leaves finely chopped

Freshly ground black pepper

1 cup good-quality chicken stock, preferably homemade

½ cup fresh lemon juice

2 tablespoons unsalted butter

½ cup grated Pecorino Romano

1 Fill a 6-quart pot with water. Bring it to a boil and add 2 tablespoons of salt. Heat ¼ cup of the olive oil in a large, heavy pot over medium-high heat. Add the cauliflower and 1 teaspoon of salt, and stir. Cook without stirring for 5 minutes. Stir, then cook the cauliflower for 5 minutes more, until golden brown but not burnt. Transfer the cauliflower to a bowl.

2 Add the pasta to the boiling water and cook until slightly firmer than al dente, 1 minute less than it says on the package. Drain, reserving ½ cup of cooking water.

3 While the pasta is cooking, pour the remaining olive oil into the pot you cooked the cauliflower in and decrease the heat to medium-low. Add the walnuts, garlic, zest, and chili flakes, and cook for 1 minute. Add the kale, a pinch of salt, and a few grinds of black pepper, and stir to combine. Add the stock and cook for about 5 minutes, or until the kale is soft and wilted. Return the cauliflower to the pot and add the lemon juice. Add the pasta and butter, and toss to combine, adding the cooking water if it looks dry. Top with the grated cheese.

Avocado Bacon Salad with Salsa Verde

SERVES 4 TO 6

You can find amazing avocados year-round in Northern California. I know how rare this is, because I lived in New York. Finding a decent avocado in New York can be tougher than snagging a seat on the subway during rush hour.

This salad can find a place on the table any time of the year, but it goes particularly well with the slightly heavier pasta dishes in the fall. Don't cut the avocados until you are almost ready to serve the salad, so they stay fresh and green, and be sure to have some bread nearby to soak up the extra salsa!

1 pound thick-cut bacon
1 head romaine lettuce, washed and torn into bite-sized pieces

2 large, ripe avocados, peeled, pitted, and cut into 2-inch long slices
1 cup Salsa Verde (page 161)
Flaky sea salt

1 Preheat the oven to 375°F.

2 Cover a baking sheet with aluminum foil, and arrange the bacon slices in a single layer. Cook for 10 minutes. Flip over and cook for another 5 minutes. Keep an eye on them! You want the bacon to be crispy but not burnt. Transfer the bacon to a plate lined with paper towels to drain. When cool, cut into 2-inch pieces.

3 Combine the lettuce, avocado, and bacon in a large mixing bowl and lightly drizzle about ½ cup of the salsa verde on top. Gently toss to combine. Serve with extra salsa verde and flaky sea salt on the side.

Fennel Salad with Grapes, Pine Nuts, and Aged Provolone

SERVES 4 TO 6

This is one of those salads that looks super fancy but only takes minutes to put together. I think it has to do with the grapes. The aged provolone provides a nice tang, so it's worth including, but if it's not available, then Grana Padano is also fine to use.

GARLIC VINAIGRETTE DRESSING

¼ cup red wine vinegar

1 clove garlic, mashed into a paste

1 tablespoon freshly squeezed lemon juice

1 teaspoon kosher salt

1 cup fruity olive oil

SALAD

2 stalks celery with leaves, stalks thinly sliced and leaves chopped

1 large fennel, stalks trimmed and bulb thinly sliced

½ pound seedless red grapes, halved

½ cup pine nuts, lightly toasted

½ cup shaved aged provolone

5 ounces wild arugula

4 ounces sopressata or salami, sliced and cut into 2-inch strips

Freshly ground black pepper

Flaky sea salt

1   To make the dressing, combine the vinegar, garlic, lemon juice, and salt in a small bowl. Slowly drizzle in the olive oil, whisking constantly to emulsify. Taste for salt, adding more if needed.

2   To assemble the salad, place all of the salad ingredients in a large mixing bowl, and toss to combine. Slowly drizzle in the dressing, a little at a time, and toss to coat the salad. You'll have some dressing left over. Sprinkle in a few grinds of black pepper and some flaky sea salt.

Crispy Potato Salad with Cranberries

SERVES 6 TO 8

I served this salad with the Radiatore with Crispy Chicken (page 56), and I swear it was better than Thanksgiving dinner. Potato salad with pasta may sound like a hard sell, but much like pesto with potatoes, it works. Slice the potatoes as thinly as possible—with a mandolin if you dare —so they become super crispy when roasting. As with anything you roast, remove as much moisture as possible to yield the most crunch. If you can't find ricotta salata, queso fresco works nicely, too.

1 pound Yukon gold potatoes, unpeeled, thinly sliced

2 tablespoons extra-virgin olive oil

Kosher salt

Freshly ground black pepper

½ head frisée, torn into bite-sized pieces

½ head oak leaf lettuce, torn into bite-sized pieces

1 cup dried cranberries

½ cup green olives, such as nocellara, pitted and halved

¾ cup finely grated ricotta salata or queso fresco

½ cup coarsely chopped fresh flat leaf parsley

Extra-virgin olive oil

Flaky sea salt

1 Preheat the oven to 375°F.

2 Pat the potatoes dry with paper towels. Place in a medium bowl and add the olive oil, 1 teaspoon of salt, and a few grinds of pepper, and toss to coat. Spread the potatoes on a rimmed baking sheet and cook for 15 minutes. Flip and cook for about 10 minutes more, or until they're browned and crisp. Remove from the oven and let cool slightly. They should be warm when you add them to the salad.

3 To assemble, combine the frisée, lettuce, cranberries, olives, cheese, and parsley in a large serving bowl. Add the potatoes to the bowl and toss to combine. Drizzle with about 3 tablespoons of fancy olive oil, season with flaky salt, and gently toss again to fully coat the salad.

Rainbow Carrots and Roasted White Beans with Bagna Cauda

SERVES 6 TO 8

I like to think of bagna cauda as the Italian equivalent of guacamole. It's savory and fatty, and I cannot stop dipping everything I see into it! If you want to get fancy, you can keep it warm with a little candle propped underneath, but I find that it stays good for quite a while without the heat. And the proper way to eat it? After dipping in a vegetable, hold a piece of bread underneath to catch the drippings!

1 can corona, butter, or gigante beans, drained, rinsed, and dried

3 tablespoons extra-virgin olive oil, plus 1 cup, divided

Kosher salt

4 tablespoons unsalted butter

6 anchovy filets, mashed into a paste

2 cloves garlic, mashed into a paste

1 head purple cauliflower, cut into florets

1 pound rainbow carrots, peeled and cut lengthwise into 3-inch pieces

1 head romanesco, cut into florets

4 radishes, any color, sliced

4 celery stalks, halved

1 loaf Italian bread, sliced

1   Preheat the oven to 375°F.

2   Arrange the beans on a baking sheet. Drizzle 3 tablespoons of olive oil over the beans and season with 1 teaspoon of salt. Bake for 20 minutes, stirring once or twice, until crispy.

3   To make the bagna cauda, melt the butter in a small saucepan over low heat. Add the anchovies and garlic, stir, and whisk in the remaining 1 cup of oil. Keep warm over very low heat while you arrange the platter.

4   Arrange the cauliflower, carrots, romanesco, radishes, celery, and bread on a platter. Scatter the beans over the salad.

5   Warm up a small bowl by filling it with hot water and pouring it out. Pour in the bagna cauda, and place the bowl in the middle of the platter.

WINTER

Pasta Friday is made for cold winter nights, when all you want to do is drink wine and eat extra-large portions of pasta. These are the heartiest, most meat-heavy dishes in the book, which is fine, because when you're cooped up inside the house, that's all you want to eat.

If you're following along week by week, you'll find the Linguine with Dungeness Crab, Scallops, and Clams (page 94) falls right around the holidays, so you can treat your guests to the Italian tradition of the Feast of Seven Fishes!

WINTER PASTA

WINTER SALADS

Zia Bruna's Spaghetti with Meatballs

SERVES 4 TO 6

Wine Pairings

RED: big, juicy Italian Montepulciano d'Abruzzo
WHITE: full-bodied Italian pinot grigio

PASTA SHAPES: spaghettoni, chitarra, tagliatelle

SERVE WITH: grated Pecorino Romano, dried red chili flakes

Recipe Note

If you end up with extra meatballs, save them to make meatball subs with the leftover crusts from the bread.

My aunt, who we call Zia Bruna, lives in a small fishing village in Puglia called Santo Spirito. Alejandro and I showed up at her door once, unannounced, when she didn't know we were in Italy. We knocked, and Zia Bruna came out on her terrace and nearly had a heart attack when she realized who was at the door! That night she took us around the town, introduced us to panzerotti (pizza dough stuffed with cheese and sauce and then fried—it's heaven), and cooked us a meal using olive oil made from her own olives. She is the only person in the world who makes meatballs that taste like the ones my great-grandmother made.

My family has been in the United States for generations, but I still have strong ties to Italy through my zia and my cousins, Monica and Paola, who live in Milan. Paola asked me once, "Do you feel a connection to Italy?" I immediately said yes, because I do, and because of traditions like Pasta Friday, my children will, too.

SAUCE

2 tablespoons unsalted butter
2 tablespoons extra-virgin olive oil
1 large yellow onion, diced
2 cloves garlic, minced
2 tablespoons tomato paste
1 (28-ounce) can whole, peeled San Marzano tomatoes, with juices
1 (16-ounce) jar Italian tomato purée
1 teaspoon kosher salt
Freshly ground black pepper

MEATBALLS

1 loaf Italian bread, cut in half lengthwise and scooped out, crusts saved for another use
½ cup whole milk
2 teaspoons kosher salt, divided
2 pounds ground beef (no leaner than 85%)
3 cloves garlic, minced
2 large fresh eggs
1 small white onion, minced
1 cup minced fresh flat leaf parsley, plus extra for garnish
¾ cup finely grated Pecorino Romano
Freshly ground black pepper
Extra-virgin olive oil, for frying
1 pound spaghetti

1 To prepare the sauce, melt the butter in a large, heavy pot over medium heat. Add the olive oil, then add the onions. Sauté for 3 minutes, until the onions are softened but not browned. Add the

RECIPE CONTINUES ↓

garlic and cook for 1 minute. Stir in the tomato paste and cook until dark red and caramelized, about 2 minutes, stirring occasionally. Add the tomatoes and juices, breaking the tomatoes apart with your hands as you add them to the pot. Add the tomato purée, 1 teaspoon of salt, and a few grinds of pepper, and stir. When the sauce begins to boil, decrease the heat to low, cover the pot, and let the sauce simmer, stirring every few minutes, while you make the meatballs.

2 To prepare the meatballs, cut the scooped bread into small pieces, and place in a medium bowl. Pour the milk over the bread and season with 1 teaspoon of the salt. Using your hands, squeeze the bread so it fully absorbs the milk.

3 In a large mixing bowl, combine the ground beef, garlic, eggs, onions, parsley, pecorino, the remaining salt, and a few grinds of black pepper. Gently stir until just combined. Pour in the milk and bread, and gently stir again.

4 Using a ¼-cup measure, scoop out the meat and roll into balls. You should have about 21 large meatballs. (Feel free to make them smaller if you prefer.)

5 Pour the oil to ¼-inch depth in a medium skillet and heat until just before smoking (about 360°F). Add the meatballs and cook until well browned on all sides, about 10 minutes. Cut into a meatball to check for doneness, and try not to eat them all before putting them in the sauce.

6 Add the meatballs to the sauce and simmer, uncovered, until the spaghetti is ready. Taste for salt, adding more if needed.

7 Fill a 6-quart pot with water. Bring it to a boil and add 2 tablespoons of salt. Add the spaghetti and stir. Cook the spaghetti until slightly firmer than al dente, 1 minute less than it says on the package. Using tongs, transfer the pasta to the sauce to finish cooking, about 2 minutes more.

8 Top with grated cheese and more parsley. Serve family-style right from the pot!

Linguine with Dungeness Crab, Scallops, and Clams

SERVES 4 TO 6

Wine Pairings

ROSE: sparkly, vibrant brut rosé

WHITE: zesty, light-bodied Italian vermentino

PASTA SHAPES: spaghetti, fettuccine, chitarra

SERVE WITH: Lemon Breadcrumbs (page 160), dried red chili flakes

When I was a kid, Christmas Eve in my family meant fried smelts, octopus salad, and seafood pasta—the classic Feast of the Seven Fishes. Most of my Californian friends had no idea what this was, so I recreated this East Coast tradition for the Pasta Friday Holiday Party! Having exactly seven types of fish is not important, so don't stress about it. If you're determined to have all seven, then put out some bruschetta with smoked salmon and make a salad with calamari. Tradition says no meat or cheese on the table, but it's your night, so you make the rules!

½ pound Bay scallops

Kosher salt

Freshly ground black pepper

3 tablespoons unsalted butter

3 tablespoons extra-virgin olive oil

4 anchovy filets, minced

½ teaspoon dried red chili flakes

4 cloves garlic, thinly sliced

½ cup dry white wine

1 pound linguine

1½ pounds littleneck or other small clams, scrubbed

½ pound Dungeness crabmeat

½ cup coarsely chopped fresh flat leaf parsley

1 lemon, zested and quartered

1 Sprinkle the scallops all over with salt and pepper.

2 Fill a 6-quart pot with water. Bring it to a boil and add 2 tablespoons of salt. While the water is heating, melt the butter with the olive oil in a large sauté pan over medium heat. Stir in the anchovies and chili flakes and mash with a wooden spoon to dissolve the anchovies. Add the garlic and cook for 1 minute. Pour in the wine and continue cooking for 2 minutes, until it reduces slightly.

3 Place the linguine in the boiling water and cook until it's slightly firmer than al dente, 1 minute less than it says on the package. Drain, reserving 1 cup of cooking water.

4 Place the clams, in their shells, in the sauté pan, cover, and cook for 5 minutes, shaking the pan every so often. The clams should be mostly open, but if not, cook for 1 more minute. Discard any unopened clams. Add the scallops and crabmeat to the pan and cook until the scallops are cooked through, about 2 minutes. Add 1 teaspoon of salt and a few grinds of black pepper.

5 Add the pasta to the pan, with half of the reserved cooking water, and toss to combine. Add more of the remaining cooking water if the pasta is too dry. Top with the parsley, zest, and lemon quarters.

Strozzapreti with Sunday Pork Neck Ragù

SERVES 6 TO 8

Wine Pairings
RED: full-bodied, rustic Italian nebbiolo
WHITE: crisp, dry Italian verdicchio

PASTA SHAPES: cavatelli, casarecce, cavatappi

SERVE WITH: grated Parmigiano-Reggiano, dried red chili flakes

I started the Pasta Friday tradition one week after my grandmother, Louise, passed away. I can still hear her saying, "Hi Al, what are you cooking tonight?" She lived across the street from me when I was growing up and never hesitated when I ran over to her house in my pajamas and begged her to make me scrambled eggs and fried salami. This was her favorite pasta, and it's the dish that ultimately changed the course of my life.

Most butchers carry pork neck bones, even if you don't see them in the case. To be safe, call the butcher a couple of days beforehand. They can always order them for you if they don't keep them in stock.

2 pounds pork neck bones
Kosher salt
Freshly ground black pepper
¼ cup extra-virgin olive oil
1 pound mild or spicy Italian sausage links
1 large yellow onion, diced
3 cloves garlic, minced
2 tablespoons tomato paste
1 (28-ounce) can whole, peeled San Marzano tomatoes, with juices

1 (14.5 ounce) can whole, peeled San Marzano tomatoes, with juices
2 bay leaves
¾ cup finely grated Pecorino Romano, plus more for serving
1 pound strozzapreti
¼ cup chopped fresh flat leaf parsley

1 Season the pork neck bones with salt and pepper.

2 Place a large, heavy pot over medium-high heat, and add the olive oil. When the oil is hot, add the pork neck bones and sear on both sides, about 3 minutes per side, working in batches if there's not enough room in the pot. Remove the bones. Sear the sausage links next, on both sides, for a total of about 8 minutes, and remove them from the pot. Cut the sausage into ¼-inch rounds when they have cooled.

3 Add the onions to the same pot and sauté for 3 minutes, until softened but not browned. Add the garlic, and cook for 1 minute, stirring and scraping up any brown bits on the bottom of the pan.

4 Add the tomato paste, and cook until dark and caramelized, about 2 minutes, stirring occasionally. Add the tomatoes and juices, breaking apart the tomatoes as you add them to the pot. Add the pork neck bones, sausage, bay leaves, 1 teaspoon of salt, and a few grinds of black pepper. Decrease the heat to a low simmer. Cover the pot and cook for at least 1 hour, stirring occasionally.

5 Fill a 6-quart pot with water. Bring it to a boil and add 2 tablespoons of salt. While you're waiting for the water to boil, take the bones out of the sauce and, using a fork, shred the meat off the bones. Place the meat back into the sauce and discard the bones. Sprinkle the pecorino into the sauce, stir, and taste for salt, adding a little at a time if it needs more.

6 Add the pasta to the boiling water, and cook until it's slightly firmer than al dente, 1 minute less than it says on the package, then drain. Add the pasta to the pot with the sauce to finish cooking, about 2 minutes. Top with the parsley, and serve family-style straight from the pot.

Pasta al Ceppo Baked with Crab and Peppers

SERVES 6 TO 8

Wine Pairings
ROSÉ: light, slightly acidic rosé spumante
WHITE: zesty, bright German pinot blanc

PASTA SHAPES: strozzapreti, cavatelli, penne

SERVE WITH: minced fresh jalapeño peppers, lemon wedges

Pasta Friday is about family and friends making time to share a meal together. My family lives in New York, so while living in Oakland, my friends became my extended family. My parents never experienced a Pasta Friday dinner until the week I made this recipe. When they visited, I decided to make this crispy baked crab dish, because my mom loves my crab cakes and my dad can't resist a good seafood pasta. I can tell that my mom, who is a famously picky eater, liked it because she asked for seconds.

There's no cheese or mayonnaise binding this recipe together. It's packed with crabmeat, peppers, and onions, and topped with panko and Parmigiano-Reggiano. It's one of my rare exceptions to the "never combine seafood and cheese" rule. Be sure to parboil the pasta so it doesn't overcook, and serve it with plenty of extra lemon wedges.

Kosher salt

1 pound pasta al ceppo

¼ cup extra-virgin olive oil

1 large white onion, diced

2 large red bell peppers, seeds and ribs removed, diced

2 cloves garlic, minced

6 tablespoons unsalted butter

1 pound crabmeat, preferably Dungeness

Freshly ground black pepper

1 cup heavy cream

½ cup freshly squeezed lemon juice

4 teaspoons finely grated lemon zest, divided

1½ teaspoons Old Bay seasoning

1 cup panko breadcrumbs

½ cup finely grated Parmigiano-Reggiano

¼ cup chopped fresh flat leaf parsley

Lemon wedges, for serving

1   Preheat the oven to 375°F.

2   Fill a 6-quart pot with water. Bring it to a boil and add 2 tablespoons of salt. Add the pasta and stir. Parboil the pasta by cooking it for 1 minute less than half of the cooking time listed on the package. For example, if the package says 12 to 14 minutes, cook the pasta for 5 minutes. Drain.

RECIPE CONTINUES ↓

3   Meanwhile, heat the oil in a medium skillet over medium-high heat. Add the onions and 1 teaspoon of salt and sauté for 2 minutes. Add the peppers and cook for another 3 minutes, until the peppers are slightly softened. Add the garlic, stir, and cook for 2 minutes. Transfer the vegetables to a large mixing bowl.

4   Melt the butter in the same skillet over medium heat and add the crabmeat, 1 teaspoon of salt, and a few grinds of pepper. Cook for 4 minutes, stirring occasionally. Add most of the crab to the bowl with the vegetables, reserving ½ cup for later. Add the pasta, heavy cream, lemon juice, 3 teaspoons of the lemon zest, and the Old Bay seasoning, and gently stir.

5   Pour the pasta into a 9 by 13-inch lasagne pan and top with the panko and Parmigiano-Reggiano. Bake for 35 to 45 minutes, until the top is golden brown. Remove from the oven and sprinkle the parsley, reserved crab, and the remaining 1 teaspoon of lemon zest over the top.

Crispy Chickpeas with Cencioni and Sausage

SERVES 4 TO 6

Wine Pairings
RED: balanced, slightly spicy Italian sangiovese
WHITE: oaky, silky California chardonnay

PASTA SHAPES: orecchiette, cavatelli, trofie

SERVE WITH: crushed Calabrian chiles in oil, extra Homemade Breadcrumbs (page 160)

Recipe Note

Canned chickpeas work well in this dish, so there's no need to spend the time soaking and cooking dried beans.

It was my birthday, and while everyone told me I needed to let someone else do the cooking, I was thrilled to watch friends and family enjoy my food. Plus, Pam came over to cook with me—the same Pam from Pam's Pasta with Sausage, Tomatoes, and Peaches (page 23).

Roasted chickpeas are one of our favorites. We eat them with rice and spinach for dinner at least once a week.

6 tablespoons extra-virgin olive oil

2 cans chickpeas, drained, rinsed, and patted dry

Kosher salt

Freshly ground black pepper

1 pound mild or spicy Italian sausage, casing removed

1 pound cencioni

1 cup dry white wine

4 tablespoons unsalted butter

¾ cup finely chopped fresh sage leaves

¼ cup finely chopped fresh rosemary

3 ounces wild arugula

½ cup Homemade Breadcrumbs (page 160)

1 Heat the olive oil in a large sauté pan over medium-high heat until hot. Add the chickpeas, 2 teaspoons of salt, and a few grinds of pepper, and cook, without stirring, for 5 minutes. (Have a splatter guard handy, as they tend to pop and make a mess!) Shake the pan, and cook for another 5 minutes, until the chickpeas are golden and crunchy. Add the sausage to the pan, break it apart with a wooden spoon, and cook for 10 minutes, until the meat is browned and fully cooked, stirring occasionally.

2 While the sausage is cooking, fill a 6-quart pot with water, bring it to a boil and add 2 tablespoons of salt. Add the pasta, and cook until al dente. Drain, reserving 1 cup of cooking water. Pour the pasta back into the pot.

3 Pour the wine into a small saucepan over medium heat. Bring to a boil and reduce by one quarter. Stir in the butter, and when the butter melts, add the sage and rosemary, and turn off the heat.

4 Pour the wine sauce over the pasta, and add the arugula. Toss until the arugula is lightly wilted. Add the chickpeas and sausage, and half of the reserved cooking water, and toss again. Add a little more cooking water if it looks too dry. Transfer the pasta to a large platter and serve with the breadcrumbs scattered on top.

Garlicky Conchiglioni with Spinach and Cheese

SERVES 6 TO 8

Wine Pairings
RED: medium-bodied, fruit-forward Italian barbera
WHITE: crisp, dry Italian pinot grigio

PASTA SHAPES: paccheri, fusilli gigante, rigatoni

SERVE WITH: grated Pecorino Romano, crushed Calabrian chiles in oil

Recipe Note
Be careful not to overcook the shells, as they fall apart easily.

This pasta has a lot of sauce. For certain dishes, like pesto and carbonara, too much sauce is not ideal, but I always love extra tomato sauce, so I can sop it up with a thick slice of bread.

You can stuff and bake giant shells, but there's something special about having them swirl around in a pot of sauce with wilted spinach and melting mozzarella. When you make for a crowd, place a ladle in the big pot and let people serve themselves, like a hearty soup.

⅓ cup extra-virgin olive oil
1 large white onion, finely chopped
7 cloves garlic, minced
3 tablespoons tomato paste
2 (28-ounce) cans whole, peeled San Marzano tomatoes, with juices

6 large fresh basil leaves
Kosher salt
Freshly ground black pepper
1 pound conchiglioni
½ pound fresh spinach leaves, whole
12 ounces whole-milk mozzarella, diced

1 Heat the olive oil in a large, heavy pot over medium-high heat. Add the onions and sauté for 5 minutes, until softened and lightly browned. Add the garlic and sauté for 1 minute, stirring occasionally.

2 Stir in the tomato paste, and sauté for another 2 minutes, until the paste is dark red and caramelized. Pour in the tomatoes and juices from the cans, using your hands to break apart the tomatoes before they hit the pot. Add the basil leaves, 1 teaspoon of salt, and a few grinds of pepper. When the sauce begins to boil, decrease the heat to low and simmer for 45 minutes, uncovered, stirring occasionally.

3 When the sauce is about 15 minutes from being done, fill a 6-quart pot with water, bring it to a boil, and add 2 tablespoons of salt. Add the shells and stir. Cook the pasta until it's slightly firmer than al dente (especially for this recipe, [as the shells will fall apart if you overcook them!], and drain.

4 Add the spinach to the sauce, and stir until the leaves are covered in sauce and begin to wilt, about 2 minutes. Add the pasta and stir to combine. Add the cheese, a little at a time, stirring to prevent the cheese from clumping. Serve directly from the pot with a ladle.

Pappardelle with Roasted Pork and Mushrooms

SERVES 6 TO 8

Wine Pairings
RED: bright, light-bodied Spanish grenache
WHITE: unoaked California pinot gris

PASTA SHAPES: tagliatelle, fettuccine, linguine

SERVE WITH: grated Parmigiano-Reggiano, dried red chili flakes

Learning how to slow-cook a pork shoulder will change your cooking forever. You can use the pork in tacos, with rice and vegetables, in a sandwich—but my favorite way to use slow-cooked pork is with fat pappardelle noodles. The key is to sear the pork first. If you skip the searing, you not only miss out on the crispy exterior, but you rob the sauce of the richness from the browned bits on the bottom of the pot. It's slightly messy and smoky, but worth it.

This sauce can easily accommodate two pounds of pasta, so if you're cooking for a crowd, add more pasta and leave the rest of the ingredients the same. If not, save the extra sauce for another meal!

3 pounds boneless pork shoulder
Kosher salt
Freshly ground black pepper
6 tablespoons extra-virgin olive oil, divided
2 large leeks, white and light green parts only, finely chopped
3 cloves garlic, thinly sliced

8 ounces shiitake mushrooms, stems trimmed, cut into ½-inch strips
1 (28-ounce) can whole, peeled San Marzano tomatoes, drained, juices reserved for another use
1 pound fresh or dried pappardelle

1 Preheat the oven to 325°F.

2 Season the pork shoulder all over with salt and pepper. Heat 3 tablespoons of the olive oil in a large Dutch oven over medium-high heat. Sear the pork on all sides, about 2 minutes per side or 12 minutes total, until a golden brown crust forms.

3 Cover the pot and transfer to the oven on the middle rack. Cook for 3 to 3½ hours, until the meat easily falls apart. Remove the pork from the oven and shred it with a fork. Give the shredded pork a good stir to cover the meat in all the juices. (The pork can be prepared to this point up to 1 day before serving. Cool to room temperature in the pot, and transfer the pot to the refrigerator. Chill overnight, and remove from the refrigerator 1 hour before reheating on the stove.)

RECIPE CONTINUES ↓

4 Heat the remaining 3 tablespoons of olive oil in a large skillet. Add the leeks and a sprinkle of salt, and sauté for about 4 minutes, or until they begin to soften. Add the garlic and cook for 30 seconds. Add the mushrooms and a few grinds of black pepper. Cook for about 10 minutes, stirring occasionally, or until the mushrooms start to brown and crisp. Add the tomatoes, gently breaking them into large pieces with your hands as you add them to the pot. Decrease the heat to low and simmer the sauce while you cook the pasta.

5 Fill a 6-quart pot with water. Bring it to a boil and add 2 tablespoons of salt. Add the pasta and stir. Cook until slightly firmer than al dente, 1 minute less than it says on the package. Watch it carefully, as pappardelle overcooks quickly!

6 While the pasta is cooking, pour the mushroom sauce into the pot with the pork and gently stir to combine. Taste for salt, adding more if needed. When the pasta is ready, use tongs to transfer it directly to the pot with the pork, and gently toss. Pour onto a large platter and serve family-style with grated cheese.

Cannelloni with Swiss Chard, Ricotta, and Béchamel

SERVES 4 TO 6

Wine Pairings

RED: light-bodied, earthy Italian sangiovese

WHITE: slightly oaked, buttery California chardonnay

PASTA SHAPES: lasagna sheets, manicotti

SERVE WITH: grated Parmigiano-Reggiano, crushed Calabrian chiles in oil

Recipe note

If using regular (not the "no-boil") cannelloni or manicotti rolls, be sure to parboil them in salted water before filling them.

I used to be such a snob when it came to those no-boil lasagna sheets. If it wasn't fresh pasta, I wanted no part of it. But then I grew up and had kids and started to understand the sacrifices you make to get a meal on the table, and this isn't even a big one! Rustichella d'Abruzzo makes great no-boil cannelloni, and it saves a crazy amount of time, especially if you're making this for a crowd.

You can use chard or kale or spinach if you like. I like chard because it's not as mild as spinach or as bitter as kale, and it comes in a few pretty colors. It will make you feel like you're eating something healthy, which you are . . . it's just covered in a lot of cheese.

FILLING

2 tablespoons extra-virgin olive oil, plus extra for drizzling

3 shallots, minced

2 bunches Swiss chard, ribs removed, leaves finely chopped

Kosher salt

1 pound whole-milk ricotta

2 large fresh eggs

2 cups finely grated Parmigiano-Reggiano, divided

½ cup chopped fresh flat leaf parsley

Freshly ground black pepper

BÉCHAMEL

3½ tablespoons unsalted butter

3½ tablespoons all-purpose flour

3 cups whole milk, warm

12 ounces no-boil cannelloni rolls

1 Preheat the oven to 375°F.

2 To make the filling, in a medium skillet, heat the olive oil over medium-high heat. Add the shallots and sauté for 3 minutes, until softened. Add the chard and ½ teaspoon of salt, and cook for 5 minutes, until the chard is wilted, stirring occasionally.

RECIPE CONTINUES ↓

3 Combine the ricotta, eggs, ½ cup of the Parmigiano-Reggiano, parsley, 1 teaspoon of salt, and a few grinds of black pepper in a mixing bowl. Stir to break up the eggs and mix well. Add the cooked chard, and stir again.

4 Cut off one corner of a resealable plastic bag and spoon the filling inside (or use a pastry bag if you have one). Set aside while you make the béchamel.

5 To make the béchamel, melt the butter in a saucepan over medium-low heat. Add the flour and whisk thoroughly, including the edges of the pot. When the flour turns light brown and smells nutty, about 1 minute, decrease the heat to low. Slowly add the milk, 1 cup at a time, whisking constantly. The sauce will be thick and lumpy at first, but don't worry. Keep whisking until all of the milk is incorporated. The béchamel is done when it's thick enough to coat the back of a spoon, about 5 minutes after you add all of the milk. Add ½ teaspoon of salt and 1 cup of the Parmigiano-Reggiano, and whisk until the cheese has completely melted into the béchamel.

6 To assemble, coat the bottom of a 9 by 13-inch lasagne pan with a thin layer of the béchamel.

7 Pipe the chard filling into one cannelloni tube until it's slightly overflowing, and place the tube in the pan. Repeat until the pan is completely filled with the cannelloni. If you have extra filling, pipe some between the rolls or at the ends of the rolls.

8 Pour about 2 cups of the béchamel over the cannelloni. They should be completely covered but not swimming in the béchamel. Bake for 35 to 40 minutes. If the top is getting too brown, lightly cover it with aluminum foil.

9 Remove from the oven and sprinkle the remaining ½ cup of grated cheese on top, and drizzle with olive oil. Let it sit for about 10 minutes before serving.

Busiate with Broccoli Pesto

SERVES 4 TO 6

Wine Pairings

RED: earthy, dry Argentine Malbec

WHITE: citrusy Spanish albariño

PASTA SHAPES: whole-grain spaghetti, penne, pipette

SERVE WITH: Lemon Breadcrumbs (page 160), dried red chili flakes

I felt sorry that all winter I was stuffing my friends with slow-cooked meats and pounds of melty cheese (although they didn't seem to mind), so I lightened things up this week.

Don't worry about overcooking the broccoli in this recipe. I grew up in New York in the eighties, when everyone overcooked everything, especially vegetables. I think I'm scarred by this, because I cringe whenever I see mushy asparagus or soggy green beans, but in this pesto, soft broccoli is key. The earthy grains in the farro pasta will make this the meal your friends will want to eat after overdoing it on last week's cheesy cannelloni.

Kosher salt

1 head of broccoli, stemmed and separated into florets

1 pound farro or whole wheat busiate

2 cloves garlic, mashed into a paste

½ cup finely grated Pecorino Romano

⅓ cup pine nuts, toasted and smashed with the back of a knife

¼ cup fresh lemon juice

1 teaspoon grated lemon zest

About ¾ cup extra-virgin olive oil

1 teaspoon coarsely ground black pepper

1 Fill a 6-quart pot with water. Bring it to a boil and add 2 tablespoons of salt. Add the broccoli and cook for about 4 minutes, or until soft. With a slotted spoon, transfer the broccoli to a colander. Add the pasta to the same water and cook until al dente. Drain, reserving 1 cup of the cooking water.

2 While the pasta is cooking, finely chop the broccoli and place it in a large bowl. Add the garlic, pecorino, pine nuts, lemon juice, and lemon zest. Give it a stir, and drizzle in the olive oil until the broccoli is submerged. Add ½ teaspoon of salt and the pepper, and toss again. Taste for salt, adding more if needed.

3 Pour the pasta and half of the reserved cooking water into the bowl with the pesto and toss. Serve immediately.

Calamarata with Braised Short Ribs and Saffron

SERVES 6 TO 8

Wine Pairings
RED: medium-bodied, fruity California pinot noir
WHITE: minerally, crisp California sauvignon blanc

PASTA SHAPES: paccheri, pappardelle, tagliatelle

SERVE WITH: grated Grana Padano, crushed Calabrian chiles in oil

Do you remember when I said not to indulge the dietary restrictions of your guests at Pasta Friday dinner? Let me tell you what happened when I inadvertently broke my own rule.

I knew a few of my no-carb eating friends were coming the week I made this dish, so I purposefully didn't toss the braised short ribs with the pasta before I served it. My no-carb friends were very happy to help themselves to the mountain of meat that sat on top of the pasta. Unfortunately, my carb-eating friends were not happy when there was hardly any meat left for them to eat. The moral of the story? Always toss your pasta, and tell those no-carb eaters to BYOM.

3 pounds bone-in short ribs
Kosher salt
Freshly ground black pepper
3 tablespoons extra-virgin olive oil
4 cloves garlic, crushed
2 cups beef stock, preferably homemade

2 teaspoons crumbled saffron threads
4 tablespoons unsalted butter
2 leeks, white and light green parts only, finely chopped
1 cup heavy cream
½ cup coarsely chopped fresh flat leaf parsley
1 pound Calamarata

1 Preheat the oven to 300°F. Season the short ribs on all sides with salt and pepper.

2 Heat the olive oil in a large Dutch oven over medium-high heat. Sear the ribs on both sides until browned, about 3 minutes per side. Transfer to a plate.

3 Add the crushed garlic to the pot and cook for 30 seconds, stirring continuously, and add the stock. Return the ribs to the pot, cover, and transfer to the oven on the middle rack. Roast for 3 hours, until the meat is falling from the bones.

4 Remove the pot from the oven. Discard the fat and bones, and shred the meat. Put the meat back in the pot and stir to coat with the juices.

RECIPE CONTINUES ↓

5 Place the saffron in a small bowl with 2 tablespoons of warm water and stir to help the saffron dissolve into the water.

6 Bring a 6-quart pot of water to a boil and add 2 tablespoons of salt.

7 While you're waiting for the water to boil, melt the butter in a sauté pan over medium-high heat. Add the leeks and sauté for about 5 minutes, or until softened. Add 1 teaspoon of salt and a few grinds of black pepper. Decrease the heat to low and add the cream, saffron, and parsley. Stir, then simmer the sauce for 10 minutes.

8 Cook the pasta in the boiling water until it's slightly firmer than al dente, 1 minute less than it says on the package, and drain. Pour the pasta into the pot with the meat.

9 Pour the saffron sauce into the pot with the pasta and short ribs, and stir to combine. Transfer to a large serving dish and serve family-style.

Spicy, Cheesy Shrimp with Lanterne and Breadcrumbs

SERVES 4 TO 6

Wine Pairings

RED: dry, crisp Italian lambrusco

WHITE: refreshingly acidic Spanish albariño

PASTA SHAPES: fusilli, penne, radiatore

SERVE WITH: extra Homemade Breadcrumbs (page 160), dried red chili flakes

I agree with those who say not to mix seafood and cheese—most of the time. I do have a soft spot for shrimp parmigiana, though. When I was growing up, most of the pizzerias in New York had a shrimp parmigiana sub on the menu, which I almost always ordered. In this recipe, I don't bread and fry the shrimp, so it's lighter than a shrimp sub and quick to prepare, but I do top it with garlicky breadcrumbs to give it that satisfying crunch.

Kosher salt

¼ cup extra-virgin olive oil, plus extra for drizzling

3 anchovy filets, minced

2 tablespoons tomato paste

2 teaspoons dried red chili flakes (use 1 teaspoon if you don't like it spicy)

4 cloves garlic, minced

1 (28-ounce) can whole, peeled San Marzano tomatoes, with juices

1½ pounds medium-sized wild shrimp, deveined, shelled, tails attached

Kosher salt

1 teaspoon dried oregano

Freshly ground black pepper

1 pound lanterne

12 ounces fresh mozzarella, sliced ¼ inch thick

½ cup Homemade Breadcrumbs (page 160)

1 Preheat the broiler.

2 Fill a 6-quart pot with water. Bring it to a boil and add 2 tablespoons of salt. While the water is coming to a boil, heat the olive oil in a large sauté pan over medium heat. Add the anchovies, tomato paste, and chili flakes, and mash with a wooden spoon. Cook for about 2 minutes, stirring occasionally, until the paste darkens and caramelizes. Add the garlic and cook for another 30 seconds. Add the can of whole tomatoes with the juices, breaking apart the tomatoes into small pieces with your hands as you add them to the pan. Add 1 teaspoon of salt, the oregano, and a few grinds of black pepper, and decrease the heat to low. Let it simmer while the pasta cooks.

3 Cook the pasta in the boiling water until it's slightly firmer than al dente, 1 minute less than it says on the package. Drain, then pour the pasta into the pot with the sauce and turn off the heat.

4 Pat the shrimp dry with paper towels and season them with salt and pepper. Arrange the shrimp on a baking sheet and drizzle with olive oil. Place the shrimp about 4 inches from the broiler and cook for about 2 minutes, flip them over, and broil for 1 minute more, just until they turn pink. Remove the shrimp from the oven and transfer them to the sauce.

5 Pour the pasta and the sauce into a 9 by 13-inch lasagne pan. Arrange the mozzarella slices on top, and drizzle with olive oil. Place 4 inches below the broiler for about 2 minutes, just until you see some of the cheese starting to brown. Remove from the oven and top with the breadcrumbs right before serving.

Veal Marsala with Escarole and Stringozzi

SERVES 4 TO 6

Wine Pairings
RED: balanced, acidic Oregon pinot noir
WHITE: slightly oaked California chardonnay

PASTA SHAPES: pappardelle, fettuccine, paccheri

SERVE WITH: Crispy, Spicy Prosciutto (page 161), grated Parmigiano-Reggiano

Veal Marsala is one of my mom's favorite dishes, and for years I wouldn't eat it because I wouldn't eat veal. The decision to eat meat or not is an extremely personal preference. I was a vegetarian for years, and although I eat meat now, I do my best to eat it only from sustainable farms.

Marsala sauce is tricky. Sometimes it's grainy and gummy, usually from too much uncooked flour floating in the sauce. I prefer a silky sauce with maybe too many mushrooms. You need good-quality stock for this, so buy it from your butcher or make it yourself. It's also important to buy real Marsala wine, not the fake stuff that says it's for cooking.

1 pound veal cutlets, pounded ¼ inch thick

Kosher salt

Freshly ground black pepper

1 cup all-purpose flour

5 tablespoons extra-virgin olive oil

2 shallots, finely chopped

1 pound cremini mushrooms, thinly sliced

3 cloves garlic, thinly sliced

¾ cup Marsala wine

1 cup homemade or good-quality store-bought beef stock

4 tablespoons unsalted butter, diced

1 pound stringozzi

1 head escarole, coarsely chopped

½ cup chopped fresh flat leaf parsley

1 Season the cutlets with salt and pepper, and lightly coat them in the flour.

2 Heat the olive oil in a large skillet over medium-high heat. When the oil is hot (about 360°F), fry the cutlets for about 2–3 minutes on each side, or until golden brown. Transfer them to a plate lined with paper towels, and when slightly cooled, cut them into 2-inch strips.

3 Fill a 6-quart pot with water. Bring it to a boil and add 2 tablespoons of salt.

4 Add the shallots to the same pan as the veal, and sauté for 3 minutes over medium heat, until softened. Add the mushrooms and cook for another 8 minutes, scraping up the bits on the bottom of the pan as the mushrooms release their juices. Add the garlic and cook for 1 minute more.

5 Add the Marsala and the stock and bring to a boil, then add the butter, stirring until the butter melts and forms a silky sauce. Decrease the heat to low and let the sauce simmer while you cook the pasta.

6 Add the pasta to the boiling water and cook until slightly firmer than al dente, 1 minute less than it says on the package. Drain, reserving ½ cup of the cooking water.

7 Add the escarole to the sauce and cook for 2 minutes, just until it wilts. Add the veal and parsley, and stir. Season with 1 teaspoon of salt and a few grinds of black pepper. Pour the sauce over the pasta and gently toss to combine. Add some of the reserved cooking water if it looks too dry. Transfer to a large serving dish and serve family-style.

Lentils with Buffalo Mozzarella and Roasted Peppers

SERVES 6 TO 8

A wintertime caprese to pair with wintertime pasta! You can use lentils of any color in this salad, but the darker ones look pretty against the red of the peppers, and they don't fall apart as easily as red lentils. Even so, try to slightly undercook the lentils so they stay firm. If you can't find buffalo mozzarella, fresh mozzarella will also work. Just be sure to bring it to room temperature before serving it.

Kosher salt

Freshly ground black pepper

2 cups dried black lentils, picked through for stones and rinsed

2 cloves garlic, mashed into a paste

½ cup extra-virgin olive oil, plus extra for drizzling

½ cup chopped fresh flat leaf parsley

½ cup fresh lemon juice

2 teaspoons grated lemon zest

4 ounces fresh spinach, stemmed and chopped into small pieces

6 ounces roasted red peppers (recipe on page 20 or store-bought), drained and chopped

8 ounces buffalo mozzarella, room temperature, cut into bite-sized pieces

Flaky sea salt

1   Bring a medium pot of water to a boil and add 1 tablespoon each of salt and pepper. Add the lentils and cook for 15 to 20 minutes, until softened but still firm. Drain, then rinse under cold water to stop the cooking process.

2   Combine the garlic, olive oil, parsley, lemon juice, zest, and 1 teaspoon of salt in a large bowl and whisk to combine. Add the lentils and toss to coat. Add the spinach and peppers, and toss again.

3   Pour the salad out onto a large dish or platter and top with the mozzarella. Sprinkle flaky sea salt over the salad and drizzle on about 2 tablespoons of fancy olive oil.

Winter Panzanella with Arugula and Squash

SERVES 6 TO 8

You know what's the greatest thing about big crunchy croutons in a salad? They soak up all of the dressing and juices and somehow still stay crispy! I could pick out all of the croutons and be thoroughly happy, even though everyone else would hate me. I don't mind slightly overdressing this salad so the croutons have more dressing to absorb (but be careful not to go overboard!). You can leave the anchovy paste out of the dressing if you're vegetarian—but don't skip it otherwise. I love the salty punch it adds to the whole dish.

Recipe Note

If you don't like squash, you can leave it out and the salad will still be great. Or you can add some roasted or raw carrots in its place.

1 butternut squash, peeled and seeded, diced into ½-inch cubes

2 tablespoons extra-virgin olive oil

1 teaspoon kosher salt

1 teaspoon coarsely ground black pepper

1 large bulb fennel, stalks trimmed, thinly sliced

4 ounces wild arugula

1 cup Homemade Croutons (page 160)

½ cup coarsely chopped fresh cilantro

¼ cup coarsely chopped fresh mint

¼ cup Fried Capers (page 161)

Flaky sea salt

CHAMPAGNE VINAIGRETTE

¼ cup champagne vinegar

1 tablespoon minced chives

1½ teaspoons Dijon mustard

1 teaspoon kosher salt

1 teaspoon finely grated lemon zest

½ teaspoon anchovy paste

¾ cup extra-virgin olive oil

1   Preheat the oven to 375°F. Place the butternut squash in a mixing bowl, add the olive oil, salt, and pepper, and toss to fully coat the squash. Spread the squash out on a baking sheet and cook for 20 minutes, until softened and lightly golden. Remove from the oven and cool to room temperature.

2   Combine the fennel, arugula, croutons, cilantro, mint, and capers in a large bowl, and add the cooled squash.

3   To make the dressing, whisk the vinegar, chives, mustard, salt, zest, and anchovy paste in a small mixing bowl. Slowly drizzle in the olive oil, whisking constantly to emulsify. Taste for salt.

4   Dress the salad right before serving. Slowly drizzle in about half of the dressing while gently tossing the salad with tongs. If it looks like it needs more dressing, add it slowly, making sure the salad isn't drenched. Taste for salt, and sprinkle on a little flaky sea salt if needed.

Broccoli with Bacon, Chives, and Walnuts

SERVES 6 TO 8

If we have to live without ripe tomatoes in the winter, at least we can indulge in hearty salads, right? I try to keep Pasta Friday salads simple and bright, to cut through all the carbs in the main dishes. This salad has a good amount of lime juice, but add it slowly, tasting as you go, to make sure it's not too much acid for you. I also love stuffing this salad into a jar and taking it to work for a weekday lunch!

1 large head broccoli, stemmed
8 ounces thick-cut bacon
Kosher salt
Freshly ground black pepper
1 head (3 to 4 ounces) red romaine lettuce, torn into bite-sized pieces
1 cup chopped walnuts, lightly toasted

1 tablespoon chopped fresh chives
Finely grated zest of 1 lime
4 tablespoons fresh lime juice
½ cup extra-virgin olive oil
Flaky sea salt

1   Preheat the oven to 375°F.

2   Cut the broccoli into bite-sized pieces.

3   Spread the bacon on a baking sheet, and cook for about 15 minutes, or until crispy. Transfer the bacon to a plate lined with paper towels to cool, and then coarsely chop.

4   Drain about half of the bacon fat from the baking sheet, and spread the broccoli on the tray, tossing to coat in the rendered fat. Season with ½ teaspoon of salt and a few grinds of black pepper. Cook for 15 to 20 minutes, until it's beginning to crisp and brown. Remove and let cool to room temperature.

5   Place the broccoli, bacon, romaine, walnuts, chives, and lime zest in a large mixing bowl. Drizzle half of the lime juice over the salad, toss, then drizzle half of the olive oil over the salad and toss again. Taste, and add more lime juice or olive oil if needed.

Citrus Salad with Avocado and Celery

SERVES 4 TO 6

My first winter in California was in 2008. Alejandro and I were young and between jobs—we had quit our cushy jobs in New York City and packed our car for the sunnier skies of the Bay Area. Walking around Berkeley (in t-shirts) in January, we were so surprised to see all the citrus trees in full bloom. I had no idea citrus was best in winter. I became enamored with grapefruit, which I had never really liked before. For this salad, oro blanco is the best grapefruit to use. If you can't find it, you can leave it out and use extra blood oranges.

½ cup thinly sliced red onion

1 oro blanco grapefruit

3 blood oranges

1 bunch watercress, torn

3 stalks celery, with leaves, sliced on a slight diagonal

1 avocado, pitted and thinly sliced

⅓ cup Lemon Breadcrumbs (page 160)

¼ cup salt-packed capers, rinsed, or Fried Capers (page 161)

Extra-virgin olive oil

Flaky sea salt

1 Soak the red onion in cold water for about 10 minutes and drain.

2 Trim the edges and peel the skin and white pith from the grapefruit and blood oranges. Thinly slice crosswise into coins and remove the seeds.

3 Spread the watercress on a large plate or platter. Arrange the citrus slices on top of the watercress, alternating the grapefruit and oranges.

4 Scatter the onions, celery, and avocado over the salad. Sprinkle the breadcrumbs and capers over the top. Finish the salad with a drizzle of fancy olive oil (about 2 to 3 tablespoons) and flaky sea salt.

SPRING

Spring starts early in Oakland, with alternating days of pouring rain and warm, sunny skies. It's the most vibrant season, with bright flowers and shiny green plants everywhere you look. Pasta Fridays during the spring are vibrant and green, too, with loads of snap peas, asparagus, and young spring lettuces. It's a mix of fresh vegetables and hearty sauces, because it still feels nice to be comforted on a rainy Friday night. Friends start talking about summer plans and the new school year, while the kids track mud inside after jumping in puddles. It's OK, though, and hard not to smile when everything feels so awake and new!

SPRING PASTAS

Spaghettoni with Red Pesto, Peas, and Burrata 130

Ari's Seafood Chitarra with Harissa 133

Big Fusilli with a Quick Lamb Ragù 134

Garganelli with Lemons, Mint, and Asparagus 135

Gnocchetti with Chorizo and Fried Lemon 138

Fusilli al Ferretto Primavera with 'Nduja 141

Bavette with Fiery Shrimp 143

Squid Ink Tonnarelli Puttanesca 144

Capellini Aglio Olio with Broccoli and Breadcrumbs 146

Impress-Your-Friends Fettuccine Alfredo 147

Grandma Louise's Noodle Pie 149

Gnocchi with Peas and Prosciutto 150

Paccheri with Braised Lamb and Big Beans 152

SPRING SALADS

Asparagus and Cannellini Beans with Mint and Grana Padano 155

Warm Halloumi with Endive and Sun-Dried Tomatoes 156

Crispy Green Salad with Crème Fraîche and Chiles 157

Strawberries and Feta with Balsamic Pearls 158

Spaghettoni with Red Pesto, Peas, and Burrata

SERVES 4 TO 6

Wine Pairings

RED: earthy, light-bodied French pinot noir

WHITE: slightly sweet New Zealand sauvignon blanc

PASTA SHAPES: spaghetti, chitarra, linguine

SERVE WITH: Spicy Breadcrumbs (page 160), grated Pecorino Romano

My meals are pretty messy, and my equipment is, er, rustic. So when Oakland Magazine *was sending a photographer for a photo shoot, I was terrified about how it would look in print. To make sure the focus was on the food, I needed a recipe with popping colors, with spice—and with burrata!*

Topping pasta with burrata is always a crowd-pleaser, and while it may feel like an easy cop-out, it's actually delicious! People LOVE burrata. If you're having a smaller gathering of four or six people, buy the smaller balls and, after plating the thick spaghetti, place the burrata right on top. For a big crowd, serve the pasta family-style, and break apart the bigger balls of burrata, scattering them over the big dish.

1 pound cherry tomatoes, halved crosswise

2 tablespoons extra-virgin olive oil

Kosher salt

Freshly ground black pepper

8 ounces shelled fresh peas, or thawed frozen peas

1 pound thick spaghetti

1 cup Red Pesto (recipe follows)

4 to 6 (4-ounce) balls of burrata (one for each person)

RED PESTO

2 cloves garlic

Kosher salt

½ cup blanched almonds

4 ounces oil-packed sun-dried tomatoes, drained and coarsely chopped

1 tablespoon capers

¾ cup coarsely chopped basil

¾ cup coarsely chopped mint

Extra-virgin olive oil

1 Preheat the oven to 375°F.

2 Arrange the cherry tomatoes, cut side up, on a rimmed baking sheet. Drizzle with olive oil, and season with 1 teaspoon of salt and a few grinds of black pepper. Transfer to the oven and roast for 20 minutes.

3 Remove the tray from the oven, add the peas, and gently shake around. Return the tray to the oven and cook 10 minutes more, until the tomatoes are slightly browned and releasing their juices.

4 Fill a 6-quart pot with water. Bring it to a boil and add 2 tablespoons of salt. Add the pasta and stir. Cook until slightly firmer than al dente, 1 minute less than it says on the package. Drain, reserving 1 cup of cooking water. Return the pasta to the pot.

5 Prepare the pesto using your preferred method that follows.

6 Add the pesto, tomatoes, and peas to the pasta, along with half of the reserved cooking water. Stir well, and add more of the remaining cooking water if it looks dry. Divide the pasta between serving plates (try slowly spinning the plate as you lower the pasta onto it to form a nest!). Place a burrata ball on top of the pasta on each plate and drizzle olive oil over the top.

RED PESTO

Mortar and pestle method:
Place the garlic in the mortar with a sprinkle of salt, and mash it into a paste. Add the almonds, sun-dried tomatoes, and capers, and mash. Add the basil and mint, grinding the leaves in a circular motion until they break down into small bits. When the ingredients are pounded together, stir in enough olive oil to fully saturate the pesto. Taste for salt, adding more if needed.

Food processor method:
Mash the garlic with the back of a knife or wooden spoon until it becomes a paste. Place the almonds, sun-dried tomatoes, capers, basil, and mint in the bowl of the food processor, and finely grind. Transfer the pesto to a bowl and stir in the garlic and enough olive oil to fully saturate the pesto. Taste for salt, adding more if needed.

Ari's Seafood Chitarra with Harissa

SERVES 4 TO 6

Wine Pairings
RED: fruity, slightly bubbly Italian lambrusco
WHITE: dry, crisp Washington state Riesling

PASTA SHAPES: spaghetti, linguine, fettuccine

SERVE WITH: extra harissa, extra-virgin olive oil

I learned a lot in my seven years of owning a restaurant, but the takeaways I cherish most are the relationships that were formed from it. One relationship in particular is with the people behind Zingerman's in Ann Arbor, Michigan. You may know their famous deli, or their bacon book, or their bakery; I know them from the business classes I took there (Zingtrain) and how they always treated me like family—especially Ari Weinzweig, who is CEO and co-founder. Ari is a mentor and inspiration to me, and he knows everything about everything when it comes to small-batch, artisanal food. Here Ari talks a bit about the brands he recommends for this dish:

"I use the very good bottled tomato sauces from the Mahjoub family. While most bottled sauce claims to be basically homemade, hardly any of them ever use the quality of raw ingredients I would. The Mahjoubs, though, actually mean it. These are made with all the excellent organic produce they grow on their own farm. . . . If you're buying bottled, these are definitely a good way to go. Their own organically grown tomatoes, traditionally made preserved lemons, traditionally cured (for a year) olives, sun-dried garlic, and wild capers. It's totally great fast food to me. Starts with good pasta (Martelli spaghetti or PrimoGrano chitarra), cooked very al dente. Not hard. Very fast, very, very good. Serve with some extra harissa and olive oil on the side."

Kosher salt

1 pound chitarra

1 (16-ounce) jar tomato sauce, or 2 cups homemade tomato sauce

¼ cup chopped, roasted red peppers

1 tablespoon sun-dried tomato harissa (less if you don't want it "wickedly" spicy)

1 tablespoon thinly sliced preserved lemon

2 pounds mixed seafood (such as squid, octopus, shrimp, scallops, cod, or even canned sardines or tuna)

1 Fill a 6-quart pot with water. Bring it to a boil and add 2 tablespoons of salt. Add the chitarra and cook until slightly firmer than al dente, 1 minute less than it says on the package, then drain.

2 Meanwhile, heat the tomato sauce in a large saucepan. Add the peppers, harissa, and lemons. Add the mixed seafood and simmer until the seafood is cooked through, about 5 minutes. Add the pasta to the pot, toss, and simmer until the pasta is fully cooked.

Big Fusilli with a Quick Lamb Ragù

SERVES 4 TO 6

Wine Pairings

RED: French Châteauneuf-du-Pape

WHITE: dry, crisp Italian pinot grigio

PASTA SHAPES: cavatappi, casarecce, rigatoni

SERVE WITH: grated Pecorino Romano, dried red chili flakes

Most of the meat sauces in this book take hours to cook, mainly because there's something so rewarding about watching big pieces of meat simply fall apart. But that doesn't mean quick meat sauces aren't worth making! Whipping up a quick sauce with lamb is especially satisfying, because lamb has such a rich, distinct taste, even without hours of cooking.

1 pound ground lamb
Kosher salt
Freshly ground black pepper
Extra-virgin olive oil
6 ounces guanciale or pancetta, diced
1 medium white onion, thinly sliced
2 cloves garlic, minced
1 pound ripe cherry tomatoes, halved crosswise
½ cup dry white wine
1 tablespoon chopped fresh rosemary
1 pound fusilli gigante
¾ cups freshly grated Pecorino Romano, plus extra for serving

1 Break up the lamb in a medium bowl and season with salt, pepper, and 1 tablespoon of olive oil.

2 Fill a 6-quart pot with water. Bring it to a boil and add 2 tablespoons of salt. While the water is coming to a boil, place 2 tablespoons of olive oil in a large, heavy pot over medium-high heat. Add the guanciale and cook for about 6 minutes, or until the fat has rendered but it's not too crispy. Remove from the pot with a slotted spoon and transfer to a plate.

3 Add the onions to the pot and sauté for about 3 minutes, or until softened. Add the garlic and cook for another 30 seconds. Now add the lamb and cook for 8 minutes, stirring occasionally, until it's browned and crisp. Add the tomatoes, wine, rosemary, 1 teaspoon of salt, and a few grinds of black pepper, and stir to combine. Cook for 10 minutes, until the wine has reduced by a quarter.

4 Meanwhile, cook the fusilli until al dente. Drain, reserving ½ cup of the cooking water.

5 Add the pasta, pecorino, and guanciale to the sauce, and toss. Slowly add some of the cooking water if it looks too dry. Serve family-style right from the pot.

Garganelli with Lemons, Mint, and Asparagus

SERVES 4 TO 6

Wine Pairings

WHITE: herbaceous, citrusy Italian pecorino
RED: floral, light Cerasuolo d'Abruzzo

PASTA SHAPES: busiate, bucatini, trofie

SERVE WITH: minced jalapeño peppers, grated Grana Padano

Lemons with pasta and cheese make me happy. They make me feel like I'm back on the Amalfi coast, sipping an Aperol spritz, twirling spaghetti in a bikini, while looking out at the bright blue sea. Some days, when it's pouring rain and I'm shuffling my boys to school, karate, and food shopping and I realize I didn't even change out of my pajama pants, I need this dish to keep me going!

This recipe brings that Amalfi feeling to Pasta Friday, while adding a California twist with local asparagus. If I'm making this for my family on a weeknight, I don't use the cream, so try experimenting and see which way you prefer. If you leave the cream out, just add more of the salty cooking water.

Kosher salt	Freshly ground black pepper
1 pound asparagus, ends snapped	6 tablespoons unsalted butter
¼ cup finely chopped mint	2 ripe lemons
¼ cup finely chopped cilantro	¾ cup heavy cream
¼ cup finely chopped flat leaf parsley	1 pound egg garganelli
½ cup extra-virgin olive oil	1 cup finely grated Grana Padano, plus extra for serving
	2 teaspoons grated lemon zest

1 Fill a 6-quart pot with water. Bring it to a boil and add 2 tablespoons of salt. Submerge the asparagus in the boiling water for 1 minute. Using tongs, quickly transfer the asparagus to an ice bath to stop the cooking process. When cool, cut it into 2-inch pieces. Keep the water boiling for the pasta.

2 In a medium bowl, combine the mint, cilantro, and parsley. Add the olive oil, ½ teaspoon of salt, and a few grinds of pepper, and stir. Set aside until the pasta is ready.

3 Melt the butter in a large, heavy pot over medium heat. Cut the lemons into quarters and squeeze directly into the pan, looking out for seeds. Throw the quarters into the pan, too. When the sauce starts to bubble, decrease the heat to low, add the cream and 1 teaspoon of

RECIPE CONTINUES ↓

salt, and stir. Simmer over low heat for 10 minutes while you make the pasta.

4 Add the pasta to the boiling water and stir. Cook the pasta until it's slightly firmer than al dente, 1 minute less than it says on the package. Drain, reserving ½ cup of cooking water.

5 Add the pasta, cheese, and half of the reserved cooking water to the lemon sauce, and quickly stir, letting the cheese melt into the sauce. Add the asparagus, and stir until the sauce looks silky and all the cheese is melted. Add more of the remaining cooking water if needed.

6 Pour onto a large serving plate. Sprinkle lemon zest on top and drizzle on a little of the herb sauce. Serve with the extra herb sauce on the side.

Gnocchetti with Chorizo and Fried Lemon

SERVES 4 TO 6

Wine Pairings

RED: big, peppery Spanish tempranillo

WHITE: elegant, citrusy Spanish Rueda

PASTA SHAPES: cavatelli, malloreddus, orecchiette

SERVE WITH: grated aged Manchego cheese, dried red chili flakes

When you cook for your family and friends on Fridays, you're giving them one night to let everything go and enjoy themselves. That's a big deal, because it's one night of the week when they don't have to cook, clean up, or pay for a meal—and they appreciate it. Hosting these dinners creates generous relationships, where friends offer to babysit and bring you soup when you're sick. It's not that your friends wouldn't do that anyway, but it definitely makes it more likely!

Let's talk about fried lemons for a second, because they are fantastic and as equally tasty on salads as with pasta. You can even eat the rind, so don't let people pick it apart. Make sure to use the dried, fully cooked Spanish chorizo, and not the uncooked Mexican chorizo.

Kosher salt

7 tablespoons extra-virgin olive oil, divided

1 lemon, thinly sliced crosswise, seeded

2 cans corona or butter beans, drained, rinsed, and patted dry

Freshly ground black pepper

5 ounces dried Spanish chorizo, skin removed, coarsely chopped

3 cloves garlic, minced

1 pound cherry tomatoes, halved crosswise

2 cups shelled fresh peas or thawed frozen peas

1 tablespoon thick balsamic vinegar

1 pound gnocchetti

¾ cup freshly grated Manchego

1   Bring a 6-quart pot of water to a boil and add 2 tablespoons of salt.

2   While the water is coming to a boil, heat 5 tablespoons of the olive oil in a large sauté pan over medium-high heat. When the oil is hot, add the lemon slices and fry for 2 minutes, flip, and fry for 1 minute more, until they turn light brown and begin to crisp. Turn off the heat, remove with a slotted spoon, and place on a plate lined with paper towels. Sprinkle with a pinch of salt.

3 Add the remaining 2 tablespoons of olive oil to the pan, and turn the heat back on to medium. Add the beans, season with 1 teaspoon of salt and a few grinds of pepper, and cook, without stirring, for 4 minutes. Shake the pan around, flip the beans, and cook for 1 minute more, until they have a crispy crust. Add the chorizo and garlic, stir it around, and cook for 3 more minutes. Add the tomatoes, peas, vinegar, and a few grinds of black pepper. Cook for 2 minutes, then taste for salt, adding more if needed. Turn off the heat.

4 Add the pasta to the boiling water, and cook until slightly firmer than al dente, 1 minute less than it says on the package. Drain, reserving ½ cup of the cooking water. Add the pasta back to the pot and place over low heat. Pour the sauce on top of the pasta, and toss. Cook for another 2 minutes, until the pasta is fully cooked. Transfer to a large serving dish, and top with the Manchego and fried lemon slices.

Fusilli al Ferretto Primavera with 'Nduja

SERVES 4 TO 6

Wine Pairings
RED: punchy, big Italian nebbiolo
WHITE: oaked, gently spiced Portuguese arinto

PASTA SHAPES: mafaldine, spaghettoni, bucatini

SERVE WITH: grated Pecorino Romano, crushed Calabrian chiles in oil

Come to a Pasta Friday dinner at my house, and you'll meet quite a diverse crowd of people who speak many languages: Spanish, Romanian, Farsi, Armenian, French, Swedish, and (luckily) Italian. I say luckily, because if Carlotta wasn't there, none of us would have a clue how to properly pronounce 'nduja (it's "en-DOO-ya").

'Nduja is a spicy, spreadable salami that adds a kick to eggs, vegetables, pasta, and even just plain old bread. It's bold, but the vegetables mellow out its hard edges and the cream balances it out. You can find it at specialty Italian shops, but if you don't have any luck, you can use dried chorizo in its place. This dish is good without meat, too, so feel free to omit the 'nduja for a vegetarian option.

Kosher salt
1 head broccoli, stemmed, separated into bite-sized florets
8 ounces snap peas, strings removed
8 ounces rainbow carrots, peeled, sliced lengthwise, cut into 2-inch pieces
8 ounces thick asparagus, halved lengthwise, cut into 2-inch pieces

3 tablespoons extra-virgin olive oil
1 medium white onion, halved, thinly sliced
5 ounces 'nduja
1 pound fusilli al ferretto
2 tablespoons unsalted butter
1 cup heavy cream
½ cup finely grated Asiago cheese
Freshly ground black pepper

1 Fill a 6-quart pot with water. Bring it to a boil and add 2 tablespoons of salt. Add the broccoli, snap peas, carrots, and asparagus to the pot, and blanch for 2 minutes.

2 Remove the vegetables from the pot with a slotted spoon, and quickly rinse under cold water or place in an ice bath to stop the cooking process. Keep the water boiling for the pasta.

3 Heat the olive oil in a large sauté pan over medium heat. Sauté the onions for 5 minutes, until they soften and begin to brown. Add the 'nduja to the pan, stir to break it apart, and cook 4 more minutes. Add the blanched vegetables to the pan with 1 teaspoon of salt, stir to combine, and turn off the heat.

RECIPE CONTINUES ↓

Fusilli al Ferretto Primavera with 'Nduja, CONTINUED

4 Add the fusilli to the boiling water. Cook until slightly firmer than al dente, 1 minute less than it says on the package. Drain, reserving ½ cup of cooking water. Return the pasta to the pot.

5 While the pasta is cooking, make the cheese sauce. In a small saucepan, melt the butter over low heat. Stir in the heavy cream and cook until hot. Add the grated cheese and whisk until fully melted.

6 Pour the cheese sauce and half of the reserved cooking water over the pasta and stir to coat. Add the vegetables and a few grinds of black pepper, and gently toss. Transfer the pasta to a large serving dish and serve immediately.

Bavette with Fiery Shrimp

SERVES 4 TO 6

Wine Pairings
RED: light-bodied, herbal
French grenache
WHITE: floral, aromatic
German Riesling

PASTA SHAPES: spaghetti,
linguine, chitarra

SERVE WITH: Lemon
Breadcrumbs (page 160),
lemon wedges

To me, shrimp scampi is always missing something. I love the brine, the garlic, and the way the slippery sauce coats every single strand of pasta, but I'm always left wishing it had more flavor. This version is quite spicy and completely satisfying. It's heavy on the herbs and lemon, and it's so much fun to watch people grabbing some bread with watery eyes after a spicy forkful. You can cut down on the heat, and it would still be intense in the best possible way. It's also pretty amazing with crabmeat instead of shrimp.

4 tablespoons extra-virgin olive oil, divided
¼ cup minced fresh flat leaf parsley
Kosher salt
Freshly ground black pepper
1½ pounds medium shrimp, peeled, deveined, tails removed, patted dry
1 pound bavette

4 tablespoons unsalted butter
5 cloves garlic, thinly sliced
2 cups shelled fresh peas or thawed frozen peas
1 tablespoon crushed Calabrian chiles in oil
½ cup chopped fresh cilantro
½ cup lemon juice
Lemon wedges, for serving

1 Combine the shrimp, 1 tablespoon of the olive oil, parsley, 1 teaspoon of salt, and 1 teaspoon of black pepper in a small bowl. Toss to evenly coat the shrimp.

2 Fill a 6-quart pot with water. Bring it to a boil and add 2 tablespoons of salt. Add the pasta and cook until al dente. Drain, reserving ½ cup of the cooking water.

3 While the pasta is cooking, melt the butter in a large sauté pan over medium heat, and add the remaining 3 tablespoons of olive oil. Add the garlic and cook until very light brown, about 1 minute, then add the peas, chiles, and 1 teaspoon of salt. Stir and cook for 2 minutes, then add the shrimp. Cook for 1 minute, flip, and cook for 1 minute more, until they're pink and cooked through. Add the lemon juice and stir.

4 Add the pasta to the pan. Toss, then add the cilantro and the reserved cooking water. Transfer to a large bowl and serve immediately with lemon wedges.

Squid Ink Tonnarelli Puttanesca

SERVES 4 TO 6

Wine Pairings
RED: spicy, full-bodied Italian primitivo
WHITE: dry, crisp Washington state Riesling

PASTA SHAPES: squid ink spaghetti, linguine, fettuccine

SERVE WITH: crushed Calabrian chiles in oil, grated Pecorino Romano

So here's a funny story: When I was a kid, all I ever wanted to eat was spaghetti in butter sauce. That was it, nothing else. Over time, my taste graduated to puttanesca, with its salt, brine, and kick, and from that point on, I ordered it every time my family went to the little Italian restaurant near my house in Inwood, New York.

Puttanesca comes together quickly, so it's an easy sauce to make for Pasta Friday. You can find squid ink pasta almost anywhere these days, but stay away from the inexpensive brands, as they tend to be too mild and taste like regular pasta.

Kosher salt

¼ cup extra-virgin olive oil, plus extra for drizzling

10 anchovy filets, finely chopped, divided

1 teaspoon dried red chili flakes

2 tablespoons tomato paste

1 medium white onion, diced

4 cloves garlic, thinly sliced

1 (14.5-ounce) can whole, peeled San Marzano tomatoes, with juices

1 cup chopped, pitted kalamata olives or other black olives

½ cup capers packed in salt, rinsed, dried, and chopped

½ cup chopped fresh flat leaf parsley

Freshly ground black pepper

1 pound squid ink tonnarelli

1 Fill a 6-quart pot with water. Bring it to a boil and add 2 tablespoons of salt. While the water is coming to a boil, heat the olive oil in a large sauté pan over medium heat. Add half of the anchovies and the chili flakes, and mash with a wooden spoon until the anchovies dissolve, about 1 minute. Add the tomato paste, mash it into the oil, and cook for about 2 minutes, or until the paste deepens in color and caramelizes. Add the onions and cook until softened, about 3 minutes. Add the garlic, and cook for 30 seconds more. Add the tomatoes with the juices, and decrease the heat to medium-low. Stir in the olives, capers, remaining anchovies, parsley, and a few grinds of black pepper. Keep on a low simmer until the pasta is done.

2 Add the pasta to the boiling water, stir, and cook until slightly firmer than al dente, 1 minute less than what it says on the package. Use tongs to transfer the pasta directly into the pan with the sauce. Toss, then cook until the pasta is done, another 2 minutes. Add a little of the pasta cooking water if the sauce looks too thick. Drizzle with your fancy olive oil.

Capellini Aglio Olio with Broccoli and Breadcrumbs

SERVES 4 TO 6

Wine Pairings
RED: refreshing, effervescent Italian lambrusco
WHITE: dry, citrusy Italian Soave

PASTA SHAPES: spaghetti, chitarra, bucatini

SERVE WITH: grated Parmigiano-Reggiano, dried red chili flakes

Recipe Note
Only cook capellini for 2 minutes. That's it. Get it all into the pot as quickly as you can without breaking the noodles, and 2 minutes later, use your tongs to transfer it from the water into the pan with your sauce to finish cooking.

I waited awhile before making capellini for a crowd. It's so thin, and I was afraid it would clump together into a pile of mush and dinner would be ruined. But I was determined to make it work.

Make sure you're buying bronze-cut pasta. This won't work with inexpensive brands; the noodles will fall apart. I use 6 medium cloves of garlic per 1 pound of pasta, because I like it super garlicky, but you can use less if you prefer. I also add some butter to help emulsify the sauce—it especially helps if you plan on scaling up the recipe to feed more people. If this is a quick late-night meal, you can skip the butter.

Kosher salt

3 tablespoons unsalted butter

⅓ cup extra-virgin olive oil, plus extra for drizzling

1 teaspoon red chili flakes (optional)

6 cloves garlic, thinly sliced

1 medium lemon, quartered

Freshly ground black pepper

½ cup chopped fresh flat leaf parsley

1 pound capellini

1 head broccoli, stemmed and cut into bite-sized florets

1 cup Lemon Breadcrumbs (page 160)

I Fill a 6-quart pot with water. Bring it to a boil and add 2 tablespoons of salt. Meanwhile, melt the butter in a large sauté pan (large enough to hold the broccoli and pasta), and add the olive oil. Add the chili flakes, if using, and stir for 30 seconds. Add the garlic and cook for 1 minute, then squeeze the lemon quarters into the pan (look out for seeds), and throw the quarters in, too. Season with 1 teaspoon of salt and a few grinds of black pepper. Add the parsley and turn off the heat.

2 Place the capellini in the boiling water and stir so it doesn't stick. Cook for exactly 1 minute, then throw the broccoli in. Cook for 1 minute longer, and, using tongs, transfer the pasta and broccoli to the pan with the sauce. Add about ¾ cup of the cooking water, and turn the heat to low. Give the pasta a good stir, add half of the breadcrumbs, and toss. Taste for salt, adding more if needed. You can also add more cooking water if it looks dry.

3 Pour the pasta into a large bowl, drizzle with some olive oil, and scatter the rest of the breadcrumbs on top. Serve immediately.

Impress-Your-Friends Fettuccine Alfredo

SERVES 4 TO 6

Wine Pairings
RED: rich, peppery French Syrah
WHITE: oaky, buttery California chardonnay

PASTA SHAPES: linguine, mafaldine, spaghetti

SERVE WITH: grated Parmigiano-Reggiano, dried red chili flakes

You might skip right over this recipe if I didn't mention impressing your friends, and this is not a recipe to skip over! The cool thing about this old-school Alfredo recipe, besides how delicious it is, is that you get to toss it together in front of your guests, making you look like a true pasta badass. It's not your typical restaurant Alfredo, which tends to be all cream and no flavor. This one is packed with cheese, and I throw some greens in for color. It would be great with spinach or broccoli, too!

1 pound asparagus, ends snapped, cut into 2-inch pieces
3 tablespoons extra-virgin olive oil or bacon fat (if you have any)
Kosher salt
Freshly ground black pepper

2½ cups freshly grated Grana Padano, rinds reserved
1 pound fettuccine
1 cup heavy cream, warmed
2 egg yolks
8 tablespoons unsalted butter
2 cloves garlic, grated on a microplane or minced

1 Preheat the oven to 350°F.

2 Place the asparagus, olive oil, ½ teaspoon of salt, and a few grinds of black pepper in a medium bowl and toss.

3 Spread the asparagus on a baking sheet, transfer to the oven, and cook for 5 to 6 minutes, until bright and crisp. Slide the asparagus into a bowl and set aside until the pasta is ready.

4 Turn the oven off, but place a large, deep dish inside to warm.

5 Fill a 6-quart pot with water. Bring it to a boil, then add 2 tablespoons of salt and the reserved cheese rind. Cook the fettuccine until slightly firmer than al dente, 1 minute less than it says on the package. Drain, discarding the rind, and reserve 1½ cups of cooking water.

6 Whisk the heavy cream and egg yolks in a small bowl, and add 1 teaspoon of salt and generous grinds of pepper.

RECIPE CONTINUES ↓

7   Slowly melt the butter in a small saucepan over medium-low heat. Add the garlic and cook for 30 seconds. Turn off the heat, add the egg yolk mixture, and stir to combine.

8   Remove the warmed dish from the oven and pour in the butter sauce. Add 1 cup of the reserved cooking water. Add the cheese, and whisk to combine and melt the cheese. Add the pasta and asparagus, and, using tongs, toss to coat the pasta. Add the remaining cooking water if the pasta is too dry. Taste for salt, and add more if needed. Serve immediately!

Grandma Louise's Noodle Pie

SERVES 6 TO 8

Wine Pairings
RED: effervescent, fruity
French brut rosé
WHITE: sparkly mimosas

PASTA SHAPES: spaghetti,
tagliatelle, fettuccine

SERVE WITH: extra-virgin
olive oil, grated Parmigiano-
Reggiano

Grandma Louise made her famous noodle pie every Easter morning, and it was the dish I was most excited to eat. This was her tradition, which is what Pasta Friday is all about, but the tradition doesn't have to be a Friday or at night. I've heard of people starting all kinds of fun weekly traditions, including weekend bagel brunches, Thursday taco throw-downs, Tuesday Cocktails on the Porch—the most important part is creating community, gathering with your tribe, and eating together. That's when Grandma Louise was happiest.

This pie gets crispy on top and stays lusciously soft on the inside, with all of the cheeses melting into each other. You can leave out the sopressata for a vegetarian option and it will still be delicious. Grandma would always make it both ways.

Kosher salt
1 pound wide egg noodles
6 large fresh eggs, beaten
6 ounces sopressata or salami, thinly sliced and cut into 2-inch pieces

2½ cups grated scarmoza (smoked mozzarella) or provolone
2 cups freshly grated Parmigiano-Reggiano, divided
Freshly ground black pepper
1¼ cups whole milk
Butter, for greasing

1 Preheat the oven to 400°F.

2 Bring a 6-quart pot of water to a boil and add 2 tablespoons of salt. Parboil the noodles by cooking them for 1 minute less than half of the time listed on the package. For example, if the package says 12 to 14 minutes, cook the pasta for 5 minutes. Drain.

3 In a large mixing bowl, combine the noodles, eggs, sopressata, scarmoza, 1 cup of the Parmigiano-Reggiano, a few grinds of pepper, and the milk, and stir.

4 Grease the bottom and sides of a 9 by 13-inch baking dish with butter. Pour the noodles into the dish, and top with the remaining Parmigiano-Reggiano. Bake for 35 to 40 minutes, until the top gets browned and crispy. Let it sit for 10 minutes before serving, or let it cool to room temperature.

Gnocchi with Peas and Prosciutto

SERVES 4 TO 6

Wine Pairings
RED: elegant, refined Italian Barolo
WHITE: balanced, silky California chardonnay

PASTA SHAPES: cavatelli, malloreddus, trofie

SERVE WITH: grated Pecorino Romano, dried red chili flakes

Recipe Note
Make things easy on yourself and buy the gnocchi if you're cooking for a crowd, and your friends will not think any less of you.

This is one of those beautifully simple dishes disguised as something much more complex.

You can go all out and make your own gnocchi. In fact, that's exactly what I did. My friend Stephanie and I spent the entire day rolling out gnocchi for thirty people according to her grandmother's recipe, and I can tell you that while it was fantastic, I will never do it again—or at least not while I'm chasing after two wild little boys and getting the house ready for guests.

Kosher salt

3 tablespoons extra-virgin olive oil, plus extra for drizzling

1 large onion, thinly sliced, cut into 2-inch strips

2 cups shelled fresh peas or thawed frozen peas

6 ounces thinly sliced prosciutto, cut into 2-inch strips

6 tablespoons salted butter

1 teaspoon chopped fresh thyme leaves

1½ pounds fresh or frozen gnocchi (store-bought or homemade)

1 Fill a 6-quart pot with water. Bring it to a boil and add 2 tablespoons of salt. While the water is coming to a boil, heat the olive oil in a large skillet over medium-high heat. Add the onions and sauté for 3 minutes, until softened but not browned. Add the peas and continue to cook for 2 minutes, then add the prosciutto. Stir and cook for only 2 minutes more, until the prosciutto is bright and pink. Turn off the heat.

2 To brown the butter, place it in a small saucepan over medium-low heat. As the butter slowly melts, swirl the pan to prevent burning. When the butter is melted, continue cooking while you gently stir. It will foam, and when the foam subsides, the butter will smell nutty and toasty. As soon as you see golden brown flecks at the bottom of the pan, immediately pour the butter into a bowl to cool, then stir in the thyme. The little brown bits at the bottom are the milk solids. I like to use them, but you can strain them out if you don't like their intensity.

3 Add the gnocchi to the boiling water and cook until they float to the top. They can overcook easily, so keep an eye on them! Drain, and pour them onto a large platter.

4 Pour the butter over the gnocchi, followed by the prosciutto and peas, and gently toss. Drizzle with olive oil and serve family-style.

Paccheri with Braised Lamb and Big Beans

SERVES 6 TO 8

Wine Pairings
RED: peppery, earthy French Syrah
WHITE: unoaked, full-bodied French Chardonnay

PASTA SHAPES: pappardelle, fettuccine, calamarata

SERVE WITH: grated Pecorino Romano, crushed Calabrian chiles in oil

If you've been following this book, week by week, you did it! You cooked fifty-one pasta meals for your friends, or maybe your family, or maybe your neighbors. Whomever you cooked for, you did it. Now, think all the way back to your first Pasta Friday dinner. It was a lifetime ago, right? Think about the relationships you have now, the bonds you have created between friends who didn't know each other, and the lives you have literally changed simply by cooking dinner every Friday.

This is a pretty majestic last meal (but don't make it the last, keep cooking!), and it's the dish people will be talking about for a long time. But even more than the food, people will be talking about this extraordinary tradition you started and how much richer their lives are because of it.

5 tablespoons extra-virgin olive oil, divided, plus extra for coating the lamb shanks

3 pounds bone-in lamb shanks

Kosher salt

Freshly ground black pepper

2 cups dry red wine, like Malbec

1 tablespoon chopped fresh oregano

8 ounces pancetta, diced

2 cans corona, gigante, or butter beans, drained and rinsed

1 large white onion, finely chopped

8 ounces oil-packed sun-dried tomatoes, drained and coarsely chopped

3 cloves garlic, minced

1 pound paccheri

1 Preheat the oven to 350°F.

2 Rub olive oil all over the lamb shanks and season with salt and pepper.

3 Heat 3 tablespoons of the olive oil in a large Dutch oven over medium-high heat. Sear the shanks on all sides until golden brown, about 4 minutes per side. Work in batches if you can't fit them all in at the same time.

4 Add the wine and oregano to the pot. Cover the pot and transfer to the oven. Cook for 3 hours, until the meat is pulling away from the bones. Remove from the oven, shred the meat, and discard the bones.

5 Heat 2 tablespoons of olive oil in a large sauté pan over medium-high heat. Add the pancetta and cook for about 5 minutes, or until browned but not burnt. Remove the pancetta from the pan with a slotted spoon and add it to the pot with the lamb.

6 Add the beans to the sauté pan, and add 1 teaspoon of salt and a few grinds of pepper. Cook for 4 minutes without stirring. Toss gently and cook for another 1 to 2 minutes, until they have a golden crust. Add the onions and sauté for 3 minutes, until softened. Add the sun-dried tomatoes and garlic, and cook for another 2 minutes. Pour it into the pot with the lamb, and stir to combine. Keep it warm over low heat while you cook the pasta.

7 Fill a 6-quart pot with water. Bring it to a boil and add 2 tablespoons of salt. Add the paccheri and stir so it doesn't stick. Cook until slightly firmer than al dente, 1 minute less than it says on the package.

8 Using a slotted spoon, transfer the paccheri to the lamb ragù, carrying some of the cooking water with it. Gently toss it all together, and cook for 2 minutes longer, until the pasta is fully cooked. Serve family-style, straight from the pot.

Asparagus and Cannellini Beans with Mint and Grana Padano

SERVES 4 TO 6

The roasted beans here make an appearance in many of my recipes, and that's because I eat them. All. The. Time. I eat them with pasta, with bread, with a spoon, and my picky children eat them, too, so they're on a steady rotation at my house.

This method works great with chickpeas, corona beans, nearly any beans. You can easily make them on the stovetop, too, instead of the oven. The trick is to get the beans dry. The drier they are, the crispier they get. Leave out the anchovies if you must, but I urge you to give them a try if you're on the fence! Just buy the good anchovies from Italy or Spain (I love the brands Ortiz and Anzienda ISAI). The cheap ones are like a salty punch in the face and are what give anchovies a bad name.

1 can cannellini beans, drained and rinsed

Kosher salt

8 ounces asparagus

6 tablespoons extra-virgin olive oil, divided

Freshly ground black pepper

4 ounces wild arugula

3 ounces shaved Grana Padano or Parmigiano-Reggiano

1 cup chopped fresh mint

1 (1.6 ounce) can anchovies, drained, filets rolled into little spirals

Flaky sea salt

1 Preheat the oven to 375°F. Line a baking sheet with paper towels, and spread the beans out to dry while the oven is heating.

2 Bring a large pot of water to a boil and add 1 tablespoon of salt. Add the asparagus and blanch for 1 minute. Drain and quickly plunge the asparagus into an ice bath to cool. Cut lengthwise into 2-inch pieces.

3 Remove the paper towels and keep the beans on the baking sheet. Drizzle 3 tablespoons of olive oil over the beans, season with 1½ teaspoons of salt and a few grinds of black pepper, and toss to fully coat. Transfer to the oven and cook for 20 minutes, until browned and crisp. Remove and cool to room temperature.

4 In a large bowl, place the arugula, asparagus, cheese, mint, and beans. Right before serving, slowly drizzle in about 3 tablespoons of olive oil and gently toss. Add a little more olive oil if it looks dry.

5 Spread the salad on a large platter and scatter around the anchovies. Garnish with flaky sea salt.

Warm Halloumi with Endive and Sun-Dried Tomatoes

SERVES 4 TO 6

I swear, as soon as people heard there would be halloumi with dinner, they came in droves. I feel like halloumi is right up there with burrata, but much less trendy. Halloumi melts well, but it also magically holds its shape when warmed up, so you get this creamy, warm bite of cheese that doesn't fall apart. Halloumi isn't the easiest cheese to find, so if you don't have any luck, use fresh goat cheese instead. Be sure to warm up the cheese right before serving the salad.

3 tablespoons unsalted butter

1 cup panko breadcrumbs

Kosher salt

1 cup fresh shelled peas

8 ounces halloumi, cut into ½-inch-thick slices, room temperature

3 ounces endive, leaves separated

5 ounces sun-dried tomatoes (not oil-packed), coarsely chopped

3 ounces frisée, coarsely chopped

¼ cup sunflower seeds, salted and roasted

¼ cup coarsely chopped fresh flat leaf parsley

Extra-virgin olive oil

Flaky sea salt

Freshly ground black pepper

1 Preheat the oven to 325°F.

2 Melt the butter in a medium skillet over medium-low heat, and add the panko. Cook for 3 to 5 minutes, until light golden, stirring constantly to prevent burning. Transfer to a dish.

3 Bring a small pot of water to a boil and add 1 tablespoon of salt. Add the peas and cook for 1 minute. Quickly drain and rinse with cold water to stop the cooking process.

4 Line a baking sheet with parchment paper. Roll each slice of cheese in the panko to completely coat, and place them on the baking sheet. Bake the cheese for 5 minutes.

5 While the cheese is baking, combine the peas, endive, tomatoes, frisée, sunflower seeds, and parsley in a large mixing bowl. Slowly drizzle in about 3 tablespoons of your fancy olive oil and gently toss.

6 Spread the salad on a large serving dish or platter, and arrange the warm cheese on top. Season the salad with flaky salt and a few grinds of pepper. If it looks dry, drizzle a little more olive oil on top. Serve immediately.

Crispy Green Salad with Crème Fraîche and Chiles

SERVES 4 TO 6

Bright, crunchy spring greens go so well with pasta! I treat my salads more like vegetable side dishes, and this one is a prime example. It's not fussy, easy to make, packed with flavor, and surprisingly tasty. I often hear at Pasta Friday, "That salad was awesome! I wasn't expecting to eat so much of it!" Salads are too often an after-thought and end up as a bowl of lettuces tossed with a sugary bottled dressing. Skip the bottle. Make your own dressing or just use olive oil (as you can see, I do that a lot).

I buy the small, whole chile peppers packed in oil, so if you're inclined, you can eat one in just one bite! Leave them out if you can't take the heat, or chop them for an all-over spiciness.

DRESSING

1 small clove garlic, mashed into a paste

½ cup crème fraîche

1 tablespoon fresh lemon juice

½ teaspoon kosher salt

½ teaspoon freshly ground black pepper

¾ cup extra-virgin olive oil

SALAD

Kosher salt

8 ounces snap peas, strings removed

8 ounces green beans, trimmed

1 head red leaf lettuce, leaves torn or chopped into bite-sized pieces

4 French radishes, thinly sliced

½ cup coarsely chopped cilantro

½ cup coarsely chopped basil

½ cup coarsely chopped mint

Freshly ground black pepper

4 or 5 whole Calabrian chiles, packed in oil

Flaky sea salt

1 To make the dressing, whisk the garlic paste, crème fraîche, lemon juice, and salt in a small bowl. Slowly drizzle in the olive oil, whisking constantly to emulsify.

2 Bring a medium pot of water to a boil and add 1 tablespoon of salt. Blanch the snap peas and green beans for 1 minute. Drain, then rinse under cold water or quickly soak in an ice bath to stop the cooking process.

3 In a large bowl, combine the lettuce, radishes, cilantro, basil, mint, green beans, and snap peas. Slowly add the dressing, about 1 tablespoon at a time, just until the salad is lightly coated. Toss to combine. (Serve the rest of the dressing on the side. It's always better to underdress and let people add more.) Season with flaky sea salt, arrange the chile peppers on top (so people don't bite into one accidently!), and serve immediately.

Strawberries and Feta with Balsamic Pearls

SERVES 4 TO 6

Balsamic pearls are magical little things that are exactly as they sound—pearls of balsamic! You can find them at specialty Italian stores or online, and it's totally worth seeking them out. They look like caviar, but when you bite into one you get a burst of savory sweetness that coats whatever else is in your mouth—in this case, strawberries, mint, and feta. If you can't find the pearls, then substitute a drizzle of syrupy, thick balsamic vinegar. Please use good feta here! The inexpensive stuff will be way too salty.

2 pounds ripe strawberries, quartered
6 ounces French feta, crumbled (I like French because it's not too salty, but use whatever you like)
1 cup coarsely chopped fresh mint
1 ounce balsamic pearls
Extra-virgin olive oil
Flaky sea salt
5 ounces mixed spring greens

1 In a large bowl, combine the strawberries, feta, mint, and pearls. Slowly drizzle with about 3 tablespoons of olive oil and toss. Taste for salt, adding some flaky sea salt if needed.

2 Spread the greens out on a large platter, and drizzle on about 1 tablespoon of olive oil. Pour the strawberry mixture over the top and toss lightly. Taste for salt and sprinkle with flaky sea salt if needed. Serve with extra olive oil on the side.

EXTRAS

Pasta Friday is all about simple gatherings, which is why I never make appetizers or desserts. I do, though, have a few extras that people go crazy over. Your guests will love you even more if you master some of these easy additions!

Homemade Breadcrumbs

1 loaf bread with a soft crust, like ciabatta

4 tablespoons salted butter, melted

2 tablespoons extra-virgin olive oil

2 cloves garlic, grated

1 teaspoon kosher salt

Freshly ground black pepper

1 to 2 teaspoons dried red chili flakes (optional, for Spicy Breadcrumbs)

Preheat the oven to 350°F. Tear the bread into pieces and place in the bowl of a food processor. Pulse the bread until it's about the size of lentils (I don't like breadcrumbs that are too fine). Pour the bread into a large bowl, then add butter, olive oil, garlic, salt, a few grinds of pepper, and the dried red chili flakes, if using. Spread on a rimmed baking sheet and bake for 12 to 15 minutes, stirring once or twice, until light brown and toasty.

VARIATIONS

Lemon Breadcrumbs

Add 1 tablespoon each of grated lemon zest and fresh lemon juice to the bowl after processing the bread.

Pancetta Breadcrumbs

Heat 1 tablespoon of olive oil in a skillet over medium heat, and cook 6 ounces finely chopped pancetta until crispy. Transfer the pancetta with a slotted spoon to a plate, and add the rendered fat to the processed breadcrumbs. Bake the breadcrumbs according to the recipe above, and mix the pancetta into the breadcrumbs when finished cooking.

Green Breadcrumbs

Finely chop a handful of fresh herbs that includes one or all of the following: parsley, basil, chives, cilantro, sage, and rosemary. Mix the herbs into the breadcrumbs when finished cooking.

Homemade Croutons

The process for my croutons is similar to how I make breadcrumbs, but for croutons, I cut the crusts from the bread. No one wants a cut lip from a sharp piece of crust. Like with the breadcrumbs, experiment! Add different spices and herbs to make them your own.

1 loaf ciabatta bread

4 tablespoons salted butter, melted

2 tablespoons extra-virgin olive oil

1 teaspoon kosher salt

Freshly ground black pepper

Preheat the oven to 350°F. Cut the crusts off the bread, and tear the bread into bite-sized pieces. It's okay if they're messy pieces of different sizes. Place the torn bread into a large bowl. Add the butter, oil, salt, and a few grinds of pepper, then toss to coat the bread. Use your hands to gently squeeze the bread, so it will absorb as much of the fat as possible. Spread the croutons out onto a baking sheet and cook for 10 to 15 minutes, stirring once or twice, until they turn light brown (they'll get too hard if overcooked).

VARIATIONS

Bacon Fat Croutons

This is my first choice if I have reserved bacon fat in the house. Substitute bacon fat for the butter and try not to eat all the croutons before tossing them on a salad.

Cheesy Croutons

Finely grate about 1 cup of Parmigiano-Reggiano on the smallest side of a box grater, and mix it with the butter and bread in the bowl.

Crispy, Spicy Prosciutto

Don't use the super expensive prosciutto for this! I usually ask the butcher for prosciutto ends, because it's cheaper by the pound.

10 ounces thinly sliced prosciutto

Extra-virgin olive oil

1 to 2 teaspoons dried red chili flakes

Preheat the oven to 375°F. Arrange the prosciutto in a single layer on a baking sheet and drizzle with 1 tablespoon of olive oil. Cook for about 10 minutes, until crispy. Cool, then crumble the prosciutto with your hands, and place in a small bowl. Add the chili flakes to taste and enough olive oil to completely submerge the prosciutto (about ¾ cup), and stir.

Fried Capers

I use capers packed in salt, but the brined ones work, too. The most important thing is that they're dry before you fry them.

Extra-virgin olive oil

1 jar salt-packed capers, rinsed and dried

Pour the olive oil into a small cast-iron skillet to a depth of ¼ inch. Heat over medium-high heat until hot, and add the capers. Fry for about 90 seconds, or until the capers appear darker, hard, and crisp. If you remove them from the heat too soon, they'll be oily and mushy, so watch them carefully. Remove with a slotted spoon and let drain on a plate lined with a paper towel.

Salsa Verde

I know there are a million salsa verde recipes out there, but I promise that this one is different! I learned this technique from my good friend Janine, who grew up in South Africa and is a true international cook. If you're short on time, omit the roasted jalapeños and scallions for a simpler version of the sauce.

6 scallions, dark green parts trimmed

4 jalapeño peppers, cut in half lengthwise (take the seeds out if you don't want it spicy)

1 to 2 cups plus 1 tablespoon extra-virgin olive oil, divided

2 bunches cilantro, minced

1 bunch parsley, minced

1 bunch mint, stemmed and minced

1 clove garlic, mashed into a paste

2 teaspoons lemon juice

Kosher salt

Freshly ground black pepper

Preheat the oven broiler. Arrange the scallions and jalapeños on a baking sheet, drizzle with 1 tablespoon of olive oil, and place a few inches under the broiler. Broil until lightly charred, about 4 minutes. Remove, and when cooled, finely chop the scallions and jalapeños.

In a large bowl, combine the scallions, jalapeños, cilantro, parsley, mint, garlic, and lemon juice. Pour in enough olive oil to submerge the ingredients, 1 to 2 cups. Add ½ teaspoon of salt and a few grinds of pepper, stir, and taste for salt.

The Greenest Garlic Bread

It's a fact that butter makes the best garlic bread, right? Also, please do not skip over the part where you're supposed to mash the garlic (I know how tempting it is to skip this step in most recipes!). It's the difference between just okay garlic bread and the best garlic bread you've ever had.

6 cloves garlic

Kosher salt

Extra-virgin olive oil

5 tablespoons unsalted butter, melted

1 small bunch fresh oregano, stemmed and minced, divided

1 loaf Italian bread or ciabatta, cut in half lengthwise and into 2-inch slices crosswise

1 cup chopped fresh flat leaf parsley

2 tablespoons chopped fresh chives

1 Preheat the oven to 350°F.

2 Pound the garlic to a paste. The easiest way to pound it is with a little salt in a mortar with a pestle. You can also do it in a pinch with the back of a knife or wooden spoon.

3 Place the garlic paste in a small bowl and cover with olive oil, about 2 tablespoons. Add the butter and half of the oregano and whisk to combine. Brush or spoon both halves of the bread with the butter sauce and season with salt. Bake for 10 minutes. Remove from the oven and scatter the fresh herbs over the bread while it's still hot.

4 Cheesy Garlic Bread: After baking the bread, arrange a layer of thickly sliced fresh mozzarella on top. Place the bread under the broiler for 1 to 2 minutes, until the cheese is bubbling. Remove from the oven and scatter the herbs on top.

Basic Pesto

Mastering a good, basic basil pesto is a necessity, mainly because most of the store-bought jars are either bland or bitter. You can use a food processor—it definitely saves time—but at least try it once with a mortar and pestle. If you use a processor, make sure you mash the garlic into a paste and add it after the other ingredients are processed.

2 cloves garlic

2 big bunches fresh basil, stemmed and coarsely chopped

½ cup pine nuts, lightly toasted

½ cup finely grated Pecorino Romano

¾ to 1 cup extra-virgin olive oil

1 tablespoon fresh lemon juice

Kosher salt

Using a mortar and pestle, mash the garlic until it forms a paste. Add the basil leaves and mash until they begin to fall apart. Add the pine nuts and continue to mash. Add the cheese and mash some more. Scoop the pesto into a small bowl, and stir in the olive oil, until the pesto is completely submerged, and lemon juice. Add ½ teaspoon of salt and taste, adding more salt if needed.

ACKNOWLEDGMENTS

Like all people, my life has had many ups and downs. A significant low point happened right after I finished writing this book, when my sister lost her battle with cancer and died at the age of forty-two. The love and support of the people listed below gave me the strength I needed to bring this project, this dream, to fruition when I didn't think I could make it happen.

First and foremost, my agent, my friend, Michele Crim. Michele, you changed my trajectory and pushed me never to give up. I am so grateful to have you in my life. To my extraordinary photographer, Sara Remington, this could not have happened without you. Thank you, my friend. To the team at Andrews McMeel, especially my amazing editor Jean Lucas, thank you for believing in Pasta Friday. Thank you to Toni Tajima for the incredible design, and Jeffrey Larson, my food stylist, who made my food look almost too good to eat. *Grazie miele* to the Peduzzi family and to the Manicaretti team for their unbelievable support.

Thank you to Ari Derfel, who ignited the spark that became this book. To my Oakland friends who showed up every week, who tested my recipes, encouraged me, drank with me, laughed and cried with me (please forgive me if I forget someone!): Cheers to Claudia Hanson, Stephanie Levy, Bahareh Nowee, Marielle Lorenz, Dana Wootton, Laura Dirtadian, Holly Perez, David Eisenmann, Denise Woodward, and Karen Agresti. To Pam Mazzola, whose love and guidance got me through many dark days. To Ari Weinzweig, who inspires me and influences me maybe more than he realizes. To Suzana Liem, my best friend, for always, always being there, every single time I need her. Suzie, life is so much better because of you.

To my family: Mom, you have taught me to be strong and brave and to keep moving, no matter how painful. I love you so much, and I thank God every day to have you in my life. Dad, this book wouldn't exist if it wasn't for you. People refer to you as a king, but to me, you're my hero. You have always been my biggest inspiration. To my girls, Jasmine and Scarlet, I love you so, so much. To Aunt Lorraine, Cristina, Hernando, and Danny, I'm blessed to have you all around me.

Alejandro, my husband and soul mate. There aren't words strong enough to express my gratitude. Thank you for allowing me to ruin our house every Friday. Thank you for your undying love, for your smile, for your strong and steady shoulders that I constantly lean on. My love grows deeper every day, when I didn't think that was possible. To Nico, thank you for being born, my boy. Your empathy and kindness are examples for us all. To Luca, my beautiful boy, thank you for your hugs and kisses when I need them most.

To my beautiful sister, Lenore. I still can't believe I have to do this without you. I miss you more with every passing day. Thank you for teaching me to love deeply, to believe in myself, to never apologize for the things I want. Thank you for always knowing what to say, for being brutally honest, for laughing through all of your pain. Please keep guiding me down the right path. This one's for you, Lenore.

METRIC CONVERSIONS AND EQUIVALENTS

METRIC CONVERSION FORMULAS

To Convert	Multiply
Ounces to grams	Ounces by 28.35
Pounds to kilograms	Pounds by .454
Teaspoons to milliliters	Teaspoons by 4.93
Tablespoons to milliliters	Tablespoons by 14.79
Fluid ounces to milliliters	Fluid ounces by 29.57
Cups to milliliters	Cups by 236.59
Cups to liters	Cups by .236
Pints to liters	Pints by .473
Quarts to liters	Quarts by .946
Gallons to liters	Gallons by 3.785
Inches to centimeters	Inches by 2.54

COMMON INGREDIENTS AND THEIR APPROXIMATE EQUIVALENTS

1 cup uncooked white rice = 185 grams

1 cup all-purpose flour = 140 grams

1 stick butter (4 ounces • ½ cup • 8 tablespoons) = 110 grams

1 cup butter (8 ounces • 2 sticks • 16 tablespoons) = 220 grams

1 cup brown sugar, firmly packed = 225 grams

1 cup granulated sugar = 200 grams

Information compiled from a variety of sources, including *Recipes into Type* by Joan Whitman and Dolores Simon (Newton, MA: Biscuit Books, 1993); *The New Food Lover's Companion* by Sharon Tyler Herbst (Hauppauge, NY: Barron's, 2013); and *Rosemary Brown's Big Kitchen Instruction Book* (Kansas City, MO: Andrews McMeel, 1998).

APPROXIMATE METRIC EQUIVALENTS

Volume

¼ teaspoon	1 milliliter
½ teaspoon	2.5 milliliters
¾ teaspoon	4 milliliters
1 teaspoon	5 milliliters
1¼ teaspoon	6 milliliters
1½ teaspoon	7.5 milliliters
1¾ teaspoon	8.5 milliliters
2 teaspoons	10 milliliters
1 tablespoon (½ fluid ounce)	15 milliliters
2 tablespoons (1 fluid ounce)	30 milliliters
¼ cup	60 milliliters
⅓ cup	80 milliliters
½ cup (4 fluid ounces)	120 milliliters
⅔ cup	160 milliliters
¾ cup	180 milliliters
1 cup (8 fluid ounces)	240 milliliters
1¼ cups	300 milliliters
1½ cups (12 fluid ounces)	360 milliliters
1⅔ cups	400 milliliters
2 cups (1 pint)	460 milliliters
3 cups	700 milliliters
4 cups (1 quart)	0.95 liter
1 quart plus ¼ cup	1 liter
4 quarts (1 gallon)	3.8 liters

Weight

¼ ounce	7 grams
½ ounce	14 grams
¾ ounce	21 grams
1 ounce	28 grams
1¼ ounces	35 grams
1½ ounces	42.5 grams
1⅔ ounces	45 grams
2 ounces	57 grams
3 ounces	85 grams
4 ounces (¼ pound)	113 grams
5 ounces	142 grams
6 ounces	170 grams
7 ounces	198 grams
8 ounces (½ pound)	227 grams
16 ounces (1 pound)	454 grams
35.25 ounces (2.2 pounds)	1 kilogram

Length

⅛ inch	3 millimeters
¼ inch	6 millimeters
½ inch	1¼ centimeters
1 inch	2½ centimeters
2 inches	5 centimeters
2½ inches	6 centimeters
4 inches	10 centimeters
5 inches	13 centimeters
6 inches	15¼ centimeters
12 inches (1 foot)	30 centimeters

OVEN TEMPERATURES

To convert Fahrenheit to Celsius, subtract 32 from Fahrenheit, multiply the result by 5, then divide by 9.

Description	Fahrenheit	Celsius	British Gas Mark
Very cool	200°	95°	0
Very cool	225°	110°	¼
Very cool	250°	120°	½
Cool	275°	135°	1
Cool	300°	150°	2
Warm	325°	165°	3
Moderate	350°	175°	4
Moderately hot	375°	190°	5
Fairly hot	400°	200°	6
Hot	425°	220°	7
Very hot	450°	230°	8
Very hot	475°	245°	9

INDEX

Andrews McMeel Publishing
a division of Andrews McMeel Universal
1130 Walnut Street, Kansas City, Missouri 64106

www.andrewsmcmeel.com

www.pastafriday.com

19 20 21 22 23 TEN 10 9 8 7 6 5 4 3 2 1

ISBN: 978-1-4494-9789-7

Library of Congress Control Number: 2019937705

Editor: Jean Z. Lucas
Designer: Toni Tajima
Art Director: Julie Barnes
Photographer: Sara Remington
Food Stylist: Jeffrey Larson
Prop Stylist: Emma Star Jensen
Production Manager: Carol Coe
Production Editor: Margaret Daniels

ATTENTION: SCHOOLS AND BUSINESSES

Andrews McMeel books are available at quantity discounts
with bulk purchase for educational, business, or sales
promotional use. For information, please e-mail the
Andrews McMeel Publishing Special Sales Department:
specialsales@amuniversal.com.